JOHN STEUART CURRY AND GRANT WOOD / *A Portrait of Rural America*

JOHN STEUART CURRY
AND GRANT WOOD
A Portrait of Rural America

JOSEPH S. CZESTOCHOWSKI

University of Missouri Press

Columbia & London, 1981

With the Cedar Rapids Art Association

Introduction, catalogues raisonnés, chronology, and
bibliography, copyright © 1981 by
Joseph S. Czestochowski

This publication was drawn from an exhibit of the works
of John Steuart Curry and Grant Wood, which was funded
with the assistance of the National Endowment for the Arts.
"Revolt Against the City," by Grant Wood, is reprinted with
the permission of James M. Dennis.
"What Should the American Artist Paint?" by John Steuart Curry,
first appeared in Art Digest, September 1935.
"On Regionalism" is reprinted with the permission
of the Thomas Hart Benton Estate.

Czestochowski, Joseph S
    John Steuart Curry and Grant Wood.

    Bibliography: p. 219
    Includes index.
        1. Curry, John Steuart, 1897–1946.   2.   Wood,
Grant, 1892–1942.   3.   Regionalism in art—United
States.   4.   Social realism.   5.   Country life in
art.   I.   Title.
ND237.C88C96   760'.044997391   80-27349
ISBN 0-8262-0336-1

Photographer Credits

John W. Barry, pages 8, 16
E. Irving Blomstrom, New Britain, Conn.: Figure 42
Geoffrey Clements, Staten Island, N.Y.: Figures 2, 23, 24,
        132, 133, 145, 160
Creative Photography, Madison, Wis.: Figures 43, 44
Helga Photo Studio, Inc., New York: Figures 137, 138
George T. Henry, Cedar Rapids, Iowa: Figures 33, 98–113,
        119, 120, 125, 139–43, 148, 149, 151, 178
William S. Nixon, Wichita: Figures 60, 88
Phillips Studio, Philadelphia: Figure 34
Taylor & Dull, Inc., New York: Figures 22, 28, 36,
        37, 39, 40, 41, 45, 46, 75, 78, 89, 91, 93

Although John Steuart Curry and Grant Wood did not formally meet until the summer of 1933 at the Stone City Art Colony in Iowa, they had shared since the mid-1920s a similar subject matter and, perhaps more importantly, a sense of mission that had motivated this country's nineteenth-century landscapists. Clearly both artists believed, along with Thomas Hart Benton, their partner in the regionalist triumverate, that there was a permanence to be found in the values in rural America. However, unlike Benton, who viewed life as a historian and was most comfortable with a turn-of-the-century America, Curry and Wood found a vitality, relevance, and persistence of these values in the contemporary rural community. Finally, unlike Benton and other so-called American Scene painters like Charles Burchfield, their perspective or period of productive activity was extremely short. Both men died in the 1940s while Benton and Burchfield painted until 1975 and 1967, respectively.

In every sense, Curry and Wood gave expression to a living experience. They were products of their times, and their art narrates the frenzied transformation in American values from those of a rural community to an urban-industrial society. It was apparent that the values of the small-town island community were unable to sustain the twentieth-century challenge of industrialization, urbanization, immigration, and economic reform: however, if we accept the intense, albeit short-lived, popularity of Curry and Wood among their contemporaries, it seems plausible that their imagery provided a vehicle wherein the transition to a bureaucratic and distended society might be affected with a minimal crisis. Thus, in reaffirming the uniqueness of American culture as a social and environmental phenomenon, their imagery possessed a timeless appeal to our sense of nationalism and other universal sentiments that has not diminished in relevance during the ensuing years.

*   *   *

In this book, the best works of John Steuart Curry and Grant Wood are presented, emphasizing the role they played in twentieth-century American art. The accompanying exhibition in 1981 at the Cedar Rapids Art Center, at Wichita State University, and at the Museum of Art and Archaeology, University of Missouri-Columbia, is notable from several points of view. In themselves, these works are testimony to the continued vitality of a rural sensibility in an urban-industrial society. And, since the Cedar Rapids Art Association is recognized for its distinguished collection of Grant Wood's works, it seems appropriate that this exhibition—together with the Marvin Cone retrospective that has preceded it—help commemorate the association's seventy-fifth anniversary. In addition, this project is a result of a truly cooperative effort on the part of many persons and institutions.

The original impetus was provided by a grant from the National Endowment for the Arts and the Iowa Arts Council. Subsequent support was provided by members of the art association. Because of the fragile condition of Grant Wood's works, the exhibit was by no means comprehensive, but it and the book that accompanies it should provide a useful resource for the study and enjoyment of two of this country's most distinguished artists.

Especial thanks is due to the following individuals, who donated their time and consideration in responding to my numerous inquiries and agreed to share their collections with us: Anita Duquette, George L. McKenna, Ida Balboul, Amy Troyen, Domenic J. Iacono, Alfred T. Collett, Lisa Calden, Evan Turner, Katharine Lee Keefe, Joshua C. Taylor, Deborah R. Emont, Lowery S. Sims, Barbara S. Krulik, John Dobkin, Linda L. Ayres, John Wilmerding, Mrs. Irving Blomstrann, Thomas N. Armstrong III, James D. Burke, Richard J. Boyle, Janice Stanland, Mary Riordan, Alixe Murphy, Mrs. Irwin Strasburger, Gloria Sullivan, Joan M. Morey, Ron Tyler, Bruce Chambers, Natalie Spassky, Ann C. Madonia, Jan K. Muhlert, Norman A. Geske, Lawrence A. Fleischman, King Vidor, Clyde Singer, Millard F. Rogers, Jr., Robert D. Kinsman, John I. H. Baur, Howard Da Lee Spencer, Wanda Corn, Mrs. Nan Wood Graham, Maurine F. Newell, Courtney Donnell, George F. Neiley, Gary Hood, Martin Bush, Delbert R. Gutridge, Eileen Shepherd, Thomas P. Lee, Charles D. Long, Rachel M. Allen, Audrey Gryder, Laurence Schmeckebier, Mrs. M. P. Naud, L. G. Hoffman, Sona Johnston, Kathleen A. Erwin, R. Harman, Jack C. Spinx, Anne von Rebhan, John Coffey, Jerry L. Kearns, Mrs. Kenneth A. Anderson, Frances Follin Jones, E. John Bullard, Martin E. Petersen, William Boyce, Christopher R. Young, Deanne Cross, John B. Turner II, James Dennis, George Henry, Susan Kendall, Phillip Grace, Elizabeth Donnan, Bret Waller, John Barry, Jr., Mrs. John (Kathleen) Curry, Charles C. Eldredge, Maebetty Langdon, J. Carter Brown, Charles Parkhurst, Karel Yasko.

At the Cedar Rapids Art Center, Sherry Maurer, Marna Tellier, Marla Hursig, and Judith Moessner deserve special thanks for their contributions.

Finally, I would like to acknowledge the Cedar Rapids Art Association Board of Trustees-Directors and the many friends of the Art Center for their continued and generous support.

J.S.C.
October 22, 1980

Contents

John Steuart Curry and
Grant Wood with their
class of art students
at Stone City, Iowa.

John Steuart Curry and Grant Wood were among the first distinguished painters of the twentieth century who conveyed a strong impression of the America west of the Hudson River. Familiar figures during the 1930s in both American art and society, Curry and Wood created images that possessed timeless appeal to our sense of nationalism as well as more universal sentiments. As a result, these American Scene artists are once again receiving widespread public attention.

Accepting the thematic complexity of their work, we realize that Curry and Wood provide a vital link between the nineteenth and twentieth centuries, especially in terms of their role in the evolution of a unique American iconography. Quite recently, this subject was examined in an exhibition, The Natural Paradise, at the Museum of Modern Art. Included in the exhibition's catalogue was an essay by Robert Rosenblum, where he concluded, "it would seem that for American art, elemental nature is still a source of myth and energy." [1]

To many artists of this century, including Curry and Wood, the prevailing mood of the 1920s and 1930s prompted a retreat to certain values that had prospered between the 1820s and the 1850s.[2] Thus we encounter a thematic interest in both primeval or elemental nature and personal isolation or anonymity. As a consequence, we can find in the work of the American Scene painters—as well as in that of artists such as Marin, Dove, Wyeth, Tobey, and Hartley—a unique recurrence of various elements that had inspired the landscapists of the nineteenth century.[3]

As a movement, the American Scene is not easily defined. This is surprising, since the term infers a unified point of view. Technically, we are obliged to accept John I. H. Baur's conclusion that the term emcompasses all the works of art that reflect this native environment.[4] And yet, in 1933, the American Scene was adopted as the theme of the government recuperative programs initiated in the wake of the Great Depression.[5] Although conceived to provide individuals with work, the program by 1935 also reflected a widespread belief in the crucial role that the arts could assume in contemporary society. As such, it answered the desire for a nationalistic art that could combat the deep psychological and sociological impact of the depression.

Since the government-initiated programs existed between 1933 and 1941–1942, these years have served to designate both the predominant style and the active years of the American Scene movement. However, this neat categorization must be qualified. Although temporarily overshadowed, the innovative experiments of the modernists maintained a vitality in the work of such artists as Sheeler, Walkowitz, Dove, and Stella. In retrospect, it was also during the early 1930s that the American Scene movement was popularized and the second wave of modernizing was formulated.[6] Therefore, it is interesting to note that in 1935 not only was the Federal Art Project of the Works Projects Administration officially established, but also the Whitney Museum held a major exhibit of abstract painting in America. And, in the next year, the major exhibitions organized by Alfred Barr at the Museum of Modern Art dealt with such movements as cubism, fantastic art, and surrealism.

In this century, the American Scene movement has represented the apogee of

1. Kynaston McShine et al., *The Natural Paradise: Painting in America, 1800–1950*, p. 37.

2. John Wilmerding, *American Art*, p. 182.

3. McShine et al., *Natural Paradise*, pp. 108–27.

4. John I. H. Baur, ed., *New Art in America*, p. 22.

5. Matthew Baigell, *The American Scene: American Painting of the 1930s*, pp. 46–54. Public Works of Art Project (PWAP) established December 1933 and terminated June 1934, succeeded by the Section, which lasted until 1943. Federal Art Project of WPA established May 1935 and lasted until 1943.

6. Lloyd Goodrich and John I. H. Baur, *American Art of Our Century*, p. 49.

7. At the same time, it can be said that it emerged in the wake of the major societal transformation, lasting four decades, that began at the close of Reconstruction and ended with the conclusion of the First World War.

8. William Innes Homer, *Robert Henri and His Circle*, p. 141.

9. In his 1941 *The Hero in America*, Dixon Wecter stated, "Homage to heroes is a vital part of our patriotism. Patriotism springs traditionally from love of place; it is a filial relation toward mother country or fatherland. The earth upon which our feet are planted, from which we draw our livelihood, becomes an over-soul, the greatest hero of our national loyalties."

10. Concurrently, farm prices continued to decline until 1932 when the price of a bushel of wheat was forty-two cents, the lowest the price had been in quite some time. For further information see Dixon Wecter, *The Age of the Great Depression, 1929–1941*, first published in 1948.

11. In addition to the actual objects, it is interesting to note that when Grant Wood lectured at the American Federation of Art's Fourth Annual Regional Conference in March 1931, his topic was a new movement, regionalism.

12. Robert H. Wiebe, *The Search for Order, 1877–1920*, p. 295.

13. Oscar Handlin, *Truth in History*, pp. 53–59.

the long tradition of realism, carrying to fruition the earlier experiments in subject matter initiated by The Eight.[7] In as much, the influential teachings of Robert Henri were a crucial factor. Although echoing the sentiments of Eakins, Henri established the spirit of the American Scene movement when in 1908 he stated: "It seems that the basis of future American art lies in our artists' appreciation of the value of the human quality all about them, which is nothing more or less than seeing the truth, and then expressing it according to their individual understanding of it."[8] Thus, artists turned to their environment for inspiration and, in so doing, they lent a fresh point of view to an otherwise staid tradition.[9]

As demonstrated by the works themselves, the American Scene movement was characterized by a rich diversity of aesthetic preferences, such as those proposed by Edward Hopper and Ben Shahn. Rightly so, contemporary critics differentiated two independent and often-times rivaling tendencies within this movement. These tendencies were regionalism, a concern for the native environment, and social realism, or the expression of a broad social humanitarianism.

Because of the widespread human suffering during the early 1930s, many of the impersonal qualities that had characterized the industrial age were generally rejected. Because of the crash of 1929 and the problems during the ensuing years, people became more apt to turn to a consideration of humanity as a social phenomenon. Between 1930 and 1932, unemployment had risen from four to fourteen million, and as such it would have been difficult to react with indifference to the urban realities mirrored in the bread lines of Reginald Marsh.[10] Therefore, it is not surprising to find that when Franklin Delano Roosevelt initiated his New Deal-Federal Arts Project in 1935, the social realists dominated the American Scene movement.

In part, this conclusion is confirmed by Thomas Hart Benton's decision to leave New York in 1935 and return to Missouri, and in the next year, Curry's departure for Wisconsin. These facts substantiate Benton's claim that by this time, regionalism was an anachronism, invented and popularized by the mass media. Indeed, when further pursued, a discrepancy does exist between the actual emergence of its characteristic imagery in works of art and the time of its public acknowledgment. At least in the case of Curry and Wood, such works were being done by 1917. For that reason, it seems plausible to conclude that in contrast to the social realist aspect of American Scenism that prospered during the mid to late 1930s, regionalism was largely a phenomenon of the 1920s and early 1930s.[11] In itself, the opening of the Whitney Museum of American Art in 1931 was a response to an already active tradition in society. Therefore, a situation existed wherein the American Scene movement was affected in two steps, one of which occurred during the next decade. The characteristics of each interacted, but their strength was indicative of shifting priorities within their time frame. With this in mind, let us turn to a discussion of the 1920s.

The period of the 1920s was one of profound transition and crisis in this country.[12] In retrospect, historians view it with a curious mixture of nostalgia and repudiation. Although the complexity of these years discourages generalizations, the prevailing mood was decidedly one of mission.[13] This concept prompted a widespread interest in the nature of our society and its adaptability to the changing times. Precipitated by the disillusionment of the First World War and its shattering of Wilsonian idealism, a revival of Americanism swept the country.[14] Americans looked to the past with an earnest hope of understanding and rationalizing the present. At this same time, quest for security in a rapidly changing society sought to stress qualities of continuity and vitality.

14. Wiebe, *The Search for Order*, pp. 284–86.

This societal search for values deemed lost was nurtured by an active literature. The works of Mark Twain and Walt Whitman assumed a new popularity, and in addition to the regionalist writers at Vanderbilt University, the frontier and sectionalist theories of Frederick Jackson Turner captivated the public imagination. A similar situation existed with the equally influential *Rise of American Civilization*, by Charles A. Beard, who together with James Harvey Robinson advocated a new history that would serve reform objectives. Animated by a creed of progress, Beard and other leading historians dealt with the concept of America as a unique culture.[15] In the mid-1920s not only did articles appear interpreting our art in geographical terms, but also the already widely read Thomas Craven established the framework for a native art that was realistic in style and traditional in subject matter. Clearly, these and other efforts sought to bolster morale by emphasizing what was good about American culture and society; ultimately seeking to convey in readily understandable terms the image of a healthy America.

15. Handlin, *Truth in History*, p. 90.

The importance of the native environment was not new to American cultural thought. Popularized by the eighteenth-century English writings of Edmund Burke (1729–1797) and Archibald Alison (1757–1839), this theory in the psychology of artistic experience dealt with the intricate relationship between objects in the material world and their effect on our emotions and inner consciousness.[16] This theory elucidates an important aspect of this country's view of nature; the individual's character is closely identified with the environment.

16. The American landscape tradition was strongly influenced by this eighteenth-century English concept. The most popular works on this subject were Edmund Burke, *A Philosophical Inquiry into the Origins of Our Ideas of the Sublime and Beautiful* (1757) and Archibald Alison, *Essays on the Nature and Principle of Taste* (1790).

This concept provided justification for the existence of the Hudson River School and much of nineteenth-century American painting. Simply stated, nature was considered a source of virtue, a place to contemplate the sublime, an avenue for spiritual sustenance and, ultimately, a symbol of national vitality. Throughout this century, the message was clear: the destiny or progress of the American people and their culture was inextricably associated with the environment. The far-reaching implications of this concept are clearly evident in the inspirational image of the pioneer heading west, the striking narrative of primordial nature, and the intense feelings of nationalism that accompanied these visual metaphors.

Therefore, those nineteenth-century images conveyed a sense of national continuity, and in so doing, unified this nation at a time of stress. Similarly, the writings of the 1920s reflect the belief that art and culture function best when they reflect our native heritage and emphasize the traditional values that exemplified past achievements.

Thus, at the outset, a consideration that is crucial to our understanding of the American Scene movement is an awareness that it encompassed complex psychological and spiritual values that existed in our past and were relevant to contemporary concerns. Of particular interest is the persistence of universal themes that address the human condition and its relationship to nature. Through these associations, the uniqueness of American culture as a social and environmental phenomenon was reaffirmed.

The characteristics of Curry's and Wood's work have been delineated in numerous books, exhibitions, and critical reviews. However, with rare exceptions, the need for stylistic categorization has prevailed in their continued identification with the regionalist movement. Of greater consequence should be their affirmity for a state of mind that transcended the merely stylistic and valued thematic associations and their continuity in American art. In retrospect, a discussion of their preference should broaden our appreciation of these artists and of this pivotal phase of American aesthetic and cultural history.

Traditionally, John Steuart Curry and Grant Wood are considered part of a group of artists that included Thomas Hart Benton and, at times, Charles Burchfield. This association with regionalism was voiced publicly in the December 24, 1934, issue of *Time* and has continued unabated. In all fairness, the term is in many respects appropriate; however, it is ironic that when the article appeared, these three artists had only recently met. Their regionalist works were being done through the 1920s, and by 1934 they all had firmly established reputations with the eastern press. These circumstances support Benton's conclusion that regionalism was merely a popular anachronism, invented as a term and movement primarily by the mass media and unsubstantiated on an art historical basis. Despite these qualifications, it must be admitted that Curry was very aware of this regionalist philosophy and, being very practical, considered its potential for financial success.[17]

17. Thomas Hart Benton, "American Regionalism, a Personal History of the Movement," pp. 43–44.

Curry and Wood prospered during a period when artists manifested a common predisposition for narrative compositions. Also, artists tended to have three principal concerns: an awareness of the existing social environment, the function of art in society, and the question of how to be a major American artist.[18] It was not sufficient to be merely an artist in America; that role was precluded by the general loss of confidence in the power of the community, the renewed sense of mission, and the intensifying nationalism within the United States.

18. Brian O'Doherty, *American Makers: The Voice and the Myth*, p. 42.

One of the most vigorous spokesmen for the growing feeling of nationalism was Thomas Hart Benton. Although Benton is excluded from the accompanying exhibit and illustrations, I would be remiss to ignore his art at this point of our discussion, especially since it adds relevance to the association of Curry and Wood. Benton was articulate, argumentative, and persistent in his intents. Prolific as both an artist and writer, Benton in large measure formulated public opinion about the American Scene movement. This was due to both his public prominence and his longevity. In this regard, it is important to understand that Benton's frame of reference was national rather than regional. It is also important to remember that Benton lived thirty years longer than either Curry or Wood, a factor that was crucial to his perspective. And he harbored a strong ideological commitment to the development of an indigenous American art that broke with its colonial and European aestheticism.

A key factor to Benton's attitude was his family, well known for its government service and its crucial role in the settlement of the frontier. As such, Benton possessed a keen awareness of history and of the role played by his family in that history. Increasingly, Benton became enthralled by this country, its dreams, energies, aspirations, and at the same time, the people who labored to make it a great nation so quickly. This acknowledgment of the dignity and the value of the workers to the community is crucial to his art and can readily be found in Curry and Wood.[19]

Benton firmly shared his contemporaries' belief that good art could be created from scenes that the average American could readily understand because of direct experience. Accordingly, he explored the commonplace and, with it, the everyday processes active in an evolving society.[20] Returning to Missouri in 1935 he maintained his home there for the duration of his life, recognizing the vulnerability of American Scene painting and acknowledging the loss of a sense of movement. In spite of this, he continued to look at life as a historian, actively seeking to chronicle the human qualities of a particular time. But as a historian, it is sadly evident that Benton most cherished turn-of-the-century America.[21]

Soon after returning from his fourth trip abroad, Grant Wood exhibited his *American Gothic* at the Art Institute of Chicago.[22] The painting was an instant success because it expressed what people were thinking at the time. To this day, much of its importance rests upon the classic subject matter found in this painting rather than its technical distinction. Like the other American Scenists, Wood sought a contemporary expression of American cultural thought and succeeded in pursuing this theme with sensitivity and originality.

A brief survey of Wood's work reveals a singular interest in the rural environment. In this respect, he echoes the conflicting attitudes characterized by Edgar Lee Masters's *Spoon River Anthology* (1915), Sinclair Lewis's *Main Street* (1920), and Thornton Wilder's *Our Town* (1938). In *Spoon River Anthology* we encounter an exploitation of the darker side of the rural environment. To be sure, the pastoral qualities of the small town are conveyed and appreciated, but so are its socially and intellectually limiting aspects. It was here that Wood's bitter satire was most eloquently treated. In paintings such as *Daughters of the Revolution* and *Victorian Survival*, Wood succeeds in conveying a clever duplicity. At one and the same time, we are given not only a seemingly natural image of a protagonist but also an amusing caricature of their affected sincerity. In a sense, Wood sought to mock those who considered themselves this country's spiritual backbone—the keepers of its traditions.[23]

Curiously, this satirizing interpretation of the Midwest disappeared within a two-year period. As characterized by Thornton Wilder's play, an active nostalgia and respect for the rural community became dominant in much of Wood's subsequent work. In a very real sense, Wood sought to preserve, at least in his painting, a rural way of life that had given his existence meaning. While implying certain limitations, almost all of his works praised the hard-working farmer as a positive element in our society. The image created is optimistic, clearly seeking to emphasize what is good about this country, and thereby providing a hopeful symbol of the nation's future and a more confident cultural self-image.

Unlike Benton, Wood did not seek to create an American style nor did he seek

19. Wiebe, *The Search for Order*, p. 112.

20. Thomas Hart Benton, "An Artist's Selection, 1908–1974," p. 4.

21. See Baigell, *The American Scene*, for a further discussion of Thomas Hart Benton.

22. For an extensive discussion on Wood, the standard monograph is James M. Dennis, *Grant Wood: A Study in American Art and Culture*.

23. Baigell, *The American Scene*, p. 111.

24. Ibid.

25. Dennis, *Grant Wood*, p. 246.

26. Quoted in Baigell, *The American Scene*, p. 111.

27. See *Art Digest* 17 (15 November 1942): 23 and 17 (1 December 1942): 4.

28. For an extensive discussion on Curry, the standard monograph is Laurence E. Schmeckebier, *John Steuart Curry's Pageant of America*. Also see the special issue of the *Kansas Quarterly* 2:4 (Fall 1970) on John Steuart Curry, edited by Bret Waller.

29. Schmeckebier, *Curry's Pageant*, p. 78.

to impose his own distinctive technique on others. Rather, he sought to establish a sense of regional art centers such as the Stone City Colony, where artists could experience free from established standards and ultimately arrive at a personal vision that expressed a particular region.[24] At the same time, Wood and Curry were very conscious that they were the first distinguished artists since George Caleb Bingham to depict the neglected essence of the American Midwest as a meaningful subject in itself. Unfortunately, the Stone City Colony lasted only during the summers of 1932 and 1933, and Wood's subsequent tenure at the University of Iowa (1934–1941) did not meet his creative expectations.[25]

Throughout his life, Wood remained strongly captivated by the primal character of the landscape. On one occasion he stated, "The naked earth in its massive contours, asserts itself through anything that is laid upon it."[26] A crucial factor was the stylistic approach learned both from his deep appreciation for American folk designs and during his stay in Munich. Influenced by fifteenth- and sixteenth-century German painting, Wood adopted a similar linear precision and a careful repetition of geometric forms, arriving at a sophisticated technique of interpretive design. Wood's landscape views are disturbingly well organized; his technical design emphasizes the order and harmony of the rural community. Pleased with the result, Wood continued in this direction until his death in 1942. Although technically distinguished and clever, his works conveyed an idealized impression of a society at a time when the public increasingly preferred a direct image. Thus, his position was extremely vulnerable within the realistically oriented American Scene. This fact, as well as the backlash from Benton's abrasive attacks against the art establishment, likely resulted in the indifferent public response accorded to a retrospective of his work at the Chicago Art Institute in 1942.[27]

As Wood, Curry was a familiar figure in American society during the 1930s.[28] Of the "regionalists," Curry is probably the least problematical, and when at his best, among the most distinguished. An excellent draughtsman, he studied in Europe for less than a year, returning to New York in the late 1920s. Once there, he quickly responded to the prevailing artistic preferences and completed his classic *Baptism in Kansas* (1928) (Figure 2). Simply, Curry believed that a sincere and lasting value was to be found in the experienced realities of the basic farm existence—the religion, the physical activities, the natural sensations, and the other integral aspects of the rural community.[29] To Curry, this imagery was an immediate way to maintain traditional ties to the past. Curiously, the Midwest was his inspiration and yet, between 1919 and 1936 he lived for the most part in New York. However, he was able to convey a sense of immediacy not readily found in the stylized designs of Wood.

Curry's works were not ones of direct observation; rather he sought the synthesis of the objective and the subjective, although his *Baptism in Kansas* depicts an actual occurrence, it is doubtful that such a dramatic compositional arrangement was provided by the observed event. Nevertheless, this is a significant work for several reasons; it directed public attention to the American Scene movement, it was done before Curry returned to the Midwest after his Paris stay, and it points out the extent to which his subject matter was selected for its design potential. The year after he completed *Baptism in Kansas*, Curry completed his painting masterpiece, *The Tornado* (Figure 5). This work possesses the qualities that characterize much of Curry's art—dramatic action, lively personalities, activated space, sculptural articulation, and vibrant color. In addition to pointing out Curry's stylistic characteristics, this work established a theme that was maintained throughout his work, the historical struggle of man with nature. It is important to realize that Curry's theme was not restricted to the violent imagery in this painting or to his impressive *The Line Storm* (Figure 33). A critic described this work as follows: "In it the spirit of the artist and perhaps his generation stands disclosed, a powerful spirit born of America, inspired by America, and dedicated to American ideas and ideals, to my mind, the canvas is a historical work of art, historical in that it mirrors our contemporary will to believe in ourselves, to believe in our own resources and in our native beauty."[30] On another occasion, Curry described his imagery as follows: "Back of the historical allegory is the great backdrop of the phenomenon of nature, and to those who live and depend on the soil for life and sustenance, this phenomenon is God."[31] This statement reaffirms an important aspect of this country's view of nature; the individual's character is closely identified with the environment. Such works as *Our Good Earth* (Figure 86) and *The Valley of the Wisconsin* (Figure 95) clearly convey an image of America as a fertile land inhabited by heroic people.

During the late 1930s, Curry increasingly turned to mural work. Valuing the opportunity for social comment, especially since the subjects would be available to large segments of the public, he daringly confronted the question of equal rights in several works, which in themselves indicate his desire to expand the sphere of his effectiveness beyond a narrow regionalism. But, in spite of his aims, Curry was not able, as Benton, to convincingly interpret the past in allegorical terms. Even works such as his exquisite *John Brown* (1939) (Figure 7) remain mannered, its success due primarily to its dynamic expressiveness. In many ways, Curry was blinded by his desire to see an American renaissance in the fine arts.[32] Unfortunately, he pursued this vision with a singular determination, while at the same time, he remained largely ambivalent to the changing times. In the final analysis, Curry was at his best in works such as *Wisconsin Landscape* (1938–1939) (Figure 8), where he was able to effectively join a meaningful subject matter with a sensitive awareness of an experienced reality.[33]

Essentially, John Steuart Curry and Grant Wood were modern American painters who, like their nineteenth-century predecessors, attempted to approach a timeless American landscape in a spirit that was both new and universal. Each created a striking definition of the rural community, the sublimity of its landscape, and its relationship to their own character. To each artist, our native environment provided a vehicle to promote traditional values that prospered in the past and were relevant to the present. They transcended the limitations of European aesthetics, seeking a visual definition of America unparalleled in our history, and in so doing, inaugurated a new phase of our continuing intimacy with our surroundings. As such, the works of Curry and Wood are remarkable examples of the persistence of earlier themes in our art, and they are individual expressions of the on-going quest for a valid American iconography and mythology.

30. *Art Digest* 9 (5 February 1935): 16.

31. Schmeckebier, *Curry's Pageant*, p. 321.

32. Baigell, *The American Scene*, p. 129.

33. For further information, see Barbara Novak, *Nature and Culture: American Landscape and Painting, 1825–1875* (New York: Oxford University Press, 1980).

John Steuart Curry and Grant Wood at Stone City, Iowa.

1. John Steuart Curry, *Kansas Cornfield*, 1933, oil on canvas, 60 x 38¼ inches Wichita Art Museum, The Roland P. Murdock Collection

17

2. John Steuart Curry, *Baptism in Kansas*, 1928, oil on canvas, 40 x 50 inches
Whitney Museum of American Art, New York

3. John Steuart Curry, *The Return of Private Davis from the Argonne*, 1928–1940
Oil on canvas, 38 x 52 inches, Hirschl and Adler Galleries

4. John Steuart Curry, *Road Menders' Camp*, 1929, oil on canvas, 40⅛ x 52 inches
University of Nebraska Art Galleries, Lincoln, F. M. Hall Collection

5. John Steuart Curry, *The Tornado*, 1929, oil on canvas, 46¼ x 60½ inches
Hackley Art Gallery, Muskegon, Michigan

6. John Steuart Curry, *The Oklahoma Land Rush*, 1938, oil on canvas, 28¾ x 59¼ inches
National Gallery of Art, Washington, D.C.

7. John Steuart Curry, *John Brown*, 1939, oil on canvas, 69 x 45 inches
The Metropolitan Museum of Art, Arthur H. Hearn Fund, 1950

23

8. John Steuart Curry, *Wisconsin Landscape*, 1938–1939, oil on canvas, 42 x 84 inches
The Metropolitan Museum of Art, George A. Hearn Fund, 1942

9. Grant Wood, *Birthplace of Herbert Hoover*, 1931, oil on composition board, 30 x 40 inches
Metropolitan Museum of Art, New York, Alan Pomeroy Collins Collection

10. Grant Wood, *Stone City, Iowa*, 1930, oil on panel, 30¼ x 40 inches
Joslyn Art Museum, Omaha, Nebraska

11. Grant Wood, *Arbor Day*, 1932, oil on masonite panel, 25 x 30 inches
King Vidor, Beverly Hills, California

13. Grant Wood, *Overmantel Decoration*, 1930, oil on composition board, 42 x 65 inches (oval)
Cedar Rapids Art Center, Gift of Isabel O. Stamats in Memory of Herbert S. Stamats

12. Grant Wood, *Spring in Town*, 1941, oil on masonite, 26 x 24½ inches
Sheldon Swope Art Gallery, Terre Haute, Indiana

14. Grant Wood, *American Gothic*, 1930, oil on composition board, 30 x 25 inches The Art Institute of Chicago, Purchase

15. Grant Wood, *Dinner for Threshers*, 1934, oil on masonite panel, 20 x 80 inches
Fine Arts Museum of San Francisco, Gift of Mr. and Mrs. John D. Rockefeller III

16. Grant Wood, *Agricultural Science Murals* (sketch) for Iowa State University Library
Oil on panel, 32¾ x 47¾, Private Collection, Cedar Rapids, Iowa

17. Grant Wood, *Young Corn*, 1931, oil on masonite, 23½ x 29½ inches
Cedar Rapids Art Center, Community School District Collection

The Works of John Steuart Curry

Sue Kendall

John Steuart Curry's *Kansas Pastoral*: The Modern
American Family on the Middle Border

1. See "A Farm Boy's Wonderful Gift to Kansas: John Steuart Curry's Statehouse Murals," *Kansas City Star* (6 February 1966), pp. 1F, 7F; for a more detailed account of the events surrounding the Topeka commission, see Calder M. Pickett, "John Steuart Curry and the Topeka Murals Controversy," in Lawrence, Kansas, University of Kansas Museum of Art, *John Steuart Curry: A Retrospective Exhibition of His Work Held in the Kansas State Capitol, Topeka, October 3–November 3, 1970*, pp. 30–41. For insight into the political and ideological alliances of White, Allen, and Huxman, see Francis W. Schruben, *Kansas in Turmoil: 1930–1936* (Columbia: University of Missouri Press, 1969).

2. For a more complete description of the proposed three-part cycle, see Laurence E. Schmeckebier, *John Steuart Curry's Pageant of America*, pp. 311–30.

3. Schmeckebier, *Curry's Pageant*, p. 327.

4. Foreword written by the artist for *John Steuart Curry* (New York: American Artist Group Monograph Number 14, 1945), unpaginated.

5. For the events surrounding the creation of the new position and a description of the artist's responsibilities, see "Resident Artist: John Steuart Curry Takes Unique Post to Encourage Rural Painting," *The Literary Digest* 122: 16 (17 October 1936): 22–24; for other national coverage of his return, see "John Curry: He Paints at Wisconsin as Artist-in-Residence," *Life* 7:26 (25 December 1939): 34–37.

In the spring of 1937, a movement was begun in Kansas to bring the nationally recognized painter, John Steuart Curry, back to his home state to paint murals for the walls of the capitol building in Topeka. Backed by William Allen White of the *Emporia Gazette*, Gov. Walter A. Huxman, and former Gov. Henry J. Allen, newspaper editors Paul Jones and Jack Harris led a campaign under the auspices of the Kansas Press Association to raise a $20,000 emolument to commission the artist. In August 1937, John Steuart Curry went to Topeka to examine the walls of the capitol corridors and to study Kansas history in preparation for the mural project that would occupy the next four years of his life.[1]

Kansas Pastoral represents the final segment in Curry's three-part historical mural cycle that opened with a panel of John Brown and the advent of the Civil War and was to include a section on the life of the pioneer Kansas homesteaders.[2] The subject of *Kansas Pastoral* is described by the artist in a letter written in 1937 to accompany the oil sketches:

> On the west wall stand the ten-foot figures of the young farmer, his wife and children, and back of them the ideal unmortgaged farm home; back of that the night and evening sky. On the long wall to the south . . . a great reach of the Kansas landscape. In the foreground the Hereford bull, wheat field, feeding steers and hogs, a grain elevator, doves in Osage orange trees. Behind all these are fields of corn and grain running back to the distant hill and the setting sun framed by the great turreted cloud to the north. . . . In these panels I shall show the beauty of real things under the hand of a beneficent Nature.[3]

In 1945, Curry reflected that "the relation of man to nature and of man to man has provided me with the subject and dramatic motivation for my work."[4] These two operative relationships—of "man to nature" and of "man to man"—are simultaneously addressed in Curry's vision of rural family life in *Kansas Pastoral*.

John Steuart Curry is most often characterized as a faithful chronicler of rural life in his native state of Kansas. But despite the corn-fed public image he liked to project, Curry did not paint his images of Kansas while sitting at home on the farm. He was born on a farm near Dunavant, Kansas, but had left his home state in 1916 to pursue his art career. After seven years as an illustrator around New York, he went to Paris in 1927 to study painting. Paradoxically, it was on his return to the East Coast that he began to earn his reputation as a regionalist by painting memories of Kansas from his studio in the art colony of Westport, Connecticut. The Topeka mural commission follows closely on the artist's celebrated return to the Midwest—after almost twenty years—to accept a position with the University of Wisconsin's College of Agriculture as the nation's first artist-in-residence.[5] Curry's murals for Kansas mark a dramatic confrontation of the artist with his past—a past, both personal and historical, that had been continuously filtered through the artist's memory and through his art during those years since he had left the Kansas farm of his youth.

The most recent writing on John Steuart Curry describes his pictures as "valuable documentary," "a portrait of rural America" intended to "depict the way things really were in the Midwest of that era."[6] Indeed, from a vantage point in the present, *Kansas Pastoral* might seem a benign representation of a typical rural family enjoying a way of life we have come to associate with the great fertile heartland of America. But when measured against its own social and historical context—against the rural realities of Kansas in 1938—this painting begins to take on mythical dimensions. The fecundity and richness of the land in *Kansas Pastoral* stand in telling contrast to actual agricultural conditions in a Kansas in the grips of the Great Depression and in the wake of the drought, dust storms, and scourge of grasshoppers that had plagued the state since 1932.[7] So, too, Curry's monumental and iconic portrayal of the rural family takes on new meaning when viewed against the real and imagined fears surrounding the future of the American family in those years.

The American family had been the object of intense scrutiny by the rapidly developing fields of social sciences in the 1920s and had been found wanting. The American family, so the experts argued, had begun as a multifunctional institution in a frontier society. Its stability grew out of the integration of each member into a productive whole. At some point in the past the processes of industrialization and urbanization had robbed the family of its functions. Schools assumed the responsibilities of education, and industry usurped the preparation of food and clothing. The family, once a productive and self-sufficient institution, became with the rise of industrialization merely a consuming unit dependent upon

6. See, for example, Joseph S. Czestochowski, "John Steuart Curry's Lithographs: A Portrait of a Rural America."

7. W. F. Zornow, *Kansas: A History of the Jayhawk State* (Norman: University of Oklahoma Press, 1957), p. 256; for an overview of agricultural conditions during the depression, see W. D. Rasmussen, ed., *Agriculture in the United States: A Documentary History*, v. 3: *War, Depression, and the New Deal, 1914–1940* (New York, 1973), especially pp. 2062–2907; see also M. S. Smith, comp., *Chronological Landmarks in American Agriculture* (Washington, D.C., U.S.D.A. Information Bulletin 425, May 1979), especially pp. 32–63.

Kansas Pastoral

8. Chief among those who argued along these lines were sociologists William Ogburn and Ernest Groves. For an incisive analysis of the sociological writings of the period, see Paula Fass, *The Damned and the Beautiful* (New York, 1977), especially chapter 2; also Christopher Lasch, *Haven in a Heartless World* (New York, 1977), especially chapter 2. For the relation between changing sex roles and the family, see Peter Filene, *Him/Her/Self* (New York, 1976), especially chapter 6.

9. The President's Research Committee on Social Trends, *Recent Social Trends in the United States* (New York, 1933), 1:xlii.

10. See Bret Waller, "An Interview with Mrs. Daniel Schuster," in *John Steuart Curry: A Retrospective*, pp. 16–17.

11. See Warren Susman's introduction to *Culture and Commitment: 1929–1945*, especially pp. 13–22.

12. Karal Ann Marling's suggestions have been invaluable. I have been influenced by her richly suggestive analysis in "A Note on New Deal Iconography: Futurology and the Historical Myth," *Prospects* (New York, 1979), 4:421–40.

13. Quoted in Schmeckebier, *Curry's Pageant*, p. 327.

the services of specialized agencies.[8] The loss of these vital functions was believed by many to herald the beginning of the end of the traditional American family.

If not everyone believed the accelerating fears of the sociologists in the professional journals, similar findings reported by *Recent Social Trends in the United States*, the result of an extensive investigation conducted under the Hoover administration, were readily accessible.[9] It seems clear that the problem was before the public eye.

Given the recurring themes of violence and impending doom in much of Curry's art, such as in *Hogs Killing a Rattlesnake* (Figure 18) or *The Tornado* (Figure 5), the artist's tender portrayals of family solidarity have been seen to represent a second, somehow contradictory side to his personality.[10] But if the intrinsic meaning of Curry's family images is sought from within their own cultural context, the artist need not be so divided. Warren Susman has characterized the 1930s as "The Age of Alfred Adler." In this way, he provided a framework in which to view the kind of reassertion of primary institutions that occurred in the 1930s as an effort to adjust to or compensate for the prevailing sense of fear and shame that he locates within the period.[11] The reactions that resulted included the development of the field of professional marriage counseling in the early 1930s and the plethora of Andy Hardy-type family films emerging from Hollywood later in the decade. Taken in this larger context, Curry's optimistic family imagery should come as no surprise. His affirmations of close family ties may be seen not as a contradiction of but rather as a kind of compensation for the same sense of fear and dread of destruction that can be found in the artist's portrayal of approaching tornadoes or falling acrobats. A conflation of the parallel themes of solidarity in the family structure and the direct threat of destruction is treated metaphorically in a number of Curry's images of farm animals, such as *Coyotes Stealing a Pig* (Figure 48) or *The Hen and Hawk* (Figure 32).

If Curry's idealized families take on mythical dimensions when measured against the widespread fears and demographic indicators of the period, the agrarian utopia in *Kansas Pastoral* contains a double referent to the kind of future-oriented expression that is central to Karal Ann Marling's iconographic analysis of New Deal historical murals.[12] Curry paints the well-ordered farm of the future, improved by the very latest developments of the agricultural science that he would have known so well through his position in the University of Wisconsin's College of Agriculture and his close friendship with its chairman, Chris Christensen. Curry, himself, hints of the future when he says of the mural, "We can suppose in these panels that the farm depicted is unmortgaged, that grain and cattle prices are rising on the Kansas City and Chicago markets."[13] In fact, opposite conditions actually prevailed, as John Steuart Curry was well aware. In 1938, the artist's own father was still struggling to make a living from his own Kansas farm:

> A God-fearing man accustomed to toil, Smith Curry is still active and undiscouraged. He has had good years and bad, made money and lost it; and if, today, his orchards are barren, his barns unpainted, and his corrals empty, he will give the reasons without complaining. "The toll of the elements—five years of dreadful acts of God; no corn, no

Oil sketch of *Kansas Pastoral*

cattle; a bank failure and double liability as a stockholder; the money from my wheat crop eaten up by taxes and interest on borrowed money." [14]

14. Thomas Craven, "John Steuart Curry," p. 37.

The artist's father's portrayal is far more rooted in the realities around him than the picture John Curry portrays in *Kansas Pastoral*. In this mural, Curry paints not the struggling Kansas farm of his father, but the idealized farm of the future.

Two significant changes are made between the oil sketch and the final mural that serve to project the image even further into the future. The grain elevator of the oil sketch is of wooden frame construction, characteristic of most constructed in the early 1900s. The final mural, however, shows the modern silo style that began to replace it in the mid-1920s on the most up-to-date farms. [15] Similarly, Curry updated the finished mural by removing the windmill that had appeared in the oil sketch. The windmill had been used in Kansas since the late 1870s to harness the most plentiful commodity of the plains, wind, to produce the scantiest commodity, water, and it was a ubiquitous motif in Curry's art. By choosing to remove this potent symbol of the plains, Curry seems to imply the advent of electricity on the farm. But electricity was not typical of rural America in 1938. As late as 1940, still less than one-third of America's farms were equipped with electricity, despite the great gains made by the Rural Electrification Administration beginning in 1935. [16] *Kansas Pastoral* is not Curry's portrait of the rural life around him, but rather a hopeful projection into the future that a hostile land will be controlled by the machine.

15. See N. H. Miller, E. Langsdorf, and R. W. Richmond, *Kansas: A Pictorial History* (Topeka, Kans., 1961), p. 271.

16. Smith, *Chronological Landmarks*, pp. 54, 63; for an overview of rural electrification, see Rasmussen, *Agriculture*, pp. 2484–87.

The new agricultural technology depicted in *Kansas Pastoral* soothes the artist's own stated ambivalence toward man's dependence on a fickle and sublime nature. The power to control nature belongs to the hand that guides the machine. [17] In terms of human relationships, however, what is given with one hand is taken with the other. When the noble yeoman no longer tills his own soil, and when technology and electricity bring labor-saving appliances to the home, the rural family is ironically robbed of its productive functions in much the same way as had been the urban family of several generations earlier. The urban solution, as documented by the sociologists, had been a reorientation of the function of the family toward the emotional needs of its members—"from institution to companionship," to coin a phrase of the period. [18] In 1933 *Recent Social Trends* had voiced the hope for future family stability in this new emotive function:

17. For Curry's ambivalence about man's relation to nature, see Bret Waller, "An Interview with Mrs. John Steuart Curry," in *John Steuart Curry: A Retrospective*, p. 8; *Kansas City Star* (6 February 1966), p. 7F; Schmeckebier, *Curry's Pageant*, pp. 291–92. On technology and the pastoral ideal, see Leo Marx, *The Machine in the Garden* (New York, 1964).

18. The phrase belongs to sociologist Ernest W. Burgess; see Lasch's discussion in *Haven*, pp. 31–33.

19. President's Research Committee on Social Trends, *American Civilization Today: A Summary of Recent Social Trends*, edited for school and college use by John T. Greenan (New York, 1934), p. 72.

20. White House on Child Health and Protection, *The Adolescent in the Family*, ed. Ernest Burgess (New York, 1934), and *The Young Child in the Home*, John B. Anderson, Chairman (New York, 1936).

21. For more on the Department of Interior murals, see Schmeckebier, *Curry's Pageant*, pp. 308–11.

22. "John Curry: He Paints at Wisconsin," p. 36.

23. On the implied presence of the machine, see James M. Dennis, *Grant Wood: A Study in American Art and Culture*, pp. 216–28.

"With the weakening of economic, social, and religious bonds in the family, its stability seems to depend upon the strength of the tie of affection, . . . the joys and responsibilities of rearing children." [19]

John Steuart Curry's monumental rural family in *Kansas Pastoral* closely matches the description of the new affectionate urban family identified by a White House Conference on Child Health and Protection held in 1936, just one year before the Topeka commission. [20] Moreover, it seems clear that the artist fully understood the differences between the old order of family interaction and the new. The old family patterns appear in a mural Curry painted for the Section of Fine Arts in the new Department of Interior building in Washington, D.C. [21] *The Homestead* was completed in 1938—the same year that the artist was working on the sketches for the Topeka commission. Here Curry paints the family of a Civil War veteran that has settled along the banks of the Arkansas River in Kansas following the signing of the Homestead Act in 1862. [22] This frontier family is shown actively making a living upon the new land, building its fences and preparing its food. Mother and daughter pare potatoes near a small garden for the family meal. A young son holds the fenceposts while his father drives them into the ground. An older sister drives the wagon full of spikes while she also cares for the youngest child. Each member of this family is actively working and contributing its energies to the productive whole. In contrast, the family in *Kansas Pastoral* is no longer engaged in the activities of production and protection. The new agricultural and domestic technologies have freed this family from the necessities of work. The farmer now leans on his shovel, overlooking a farm so well ordered that it seems to run itself. The fruits of the harvest are lined up in mechanical precision as covert symbols of the new machine technology. [23] Even the hogs stand at attention in this efficient environment. The mother in *Kansas Pastoral* is no longer occupied with the task of preparing food, her only function is the giving of affection.

Curry has used the arched corridor in the middle of the wall as a compositional device to reinforce the content of his mural, as it sharply separates the

Homestead

man's world of agribusiness from the woman's sphere, dominating the home. Similarly, animal metaphors in the two murals are used to reinforce the content of the works. In *The Homestead*, rooster, chicks, and chickens peck and feed near the foreground garden as bountiful reminders of their capacity to provide this frontier family with eggs and a number of nice Sunday dinners, besides. But only one chicken appears in *Kansas Pastoral*, shown prominently in the foreground in telling juxtaposition with the Kansas mother as it forms the third point in an almost pedimental triangular composition. This single chicken is now characterized as a "mother hen," cuddling and protecting her baby chicks as she becomes an attribute figure echoing the theme of loving motherhood shown in the Kansas madonna and child.

John Steuart Curry clearly understood the historical significance of the new and old family patterns. The White House conference had established that the older, work-oriented family structure still characterized rural America in 1936. But in *Kansas Pastoral*, Curry has created his own vision for the people of Kansas. The new agricultural technology promises to overcome the destructive powers of a sublime nature. The nobel yeoman of the new order will reap a harvest of plenty without having to till the soil by the sweat of his brow. The new rural family will be freed from the necessities of labor as the machine brings leisure to the home. The various functions that had served to bind the members of the frontier family together are gradually yielded up during this transition. But the artist has compensated for the loss by introducing into his ideal rural setting those very urban, emotive, affectionate family patterns that were believed by experts of the time to hold the key to the future stability of the urban family. Thus, the stability of the rural family of the future is also assured if it turns its attention to the emotional and affectional needs of its members. In the context of Kansas in 1938, Curry's vision in this mural is clearly utopian. Both in the richness of the land and in the structure of the rural family, it comments on the present through its marked disparity to it. His message is hopeful and intended to persuade. It is, in fact, the propaganda of a new social order.[24] It is somewhat ironic that this regionalist painter's solution to the problems facing rural America is a decidedly urban one. Seen in its own context, John Steuart Curry's *Kansas Pastoral* becomes not a documentary treatment of the Kansas he saw, but rather an urbanite's projection of the rural ideal—the modern affectionate family reunited with a well-controlled land.

24. For Curry's views on propaganda and social relevance in art, see John Steuart Curry, "What Should the American Artist Paint?," originally published in *Art Digest* (September 1935): 29, which also appears in this volume; Schmeckebier, *Curry's Pageant*, pp. 291–92.

What Should the American Artist Paint?

By John Steuart Curry

The artist must paint the thing that is most alive to him. To do this in a distinguished manner takes thought and a realization of what is to be accomplished. Thousands of us are now painting what is called "the American scene." We are glorifying landscapes, elevated stations, subways, butcher shops, 14th Street, Mid-Western farmers, and we are one and all painting out of the fullness of our life and experiences.

Now, because the artist is an American and paints a sky-scraper, that will not make a great work of art, nor even a distinguished one. There must first be a lively interest in the subject; then comes the step of designing the form so that the feeling and underlying motive that comes through will be sharpened and given its full dramatic power. It is a fault that we all fall into—to paint a fact without first considering the dramatic or spiritual side of the subject. It is well to remember always that thing which is beyond the power of the camera eye to report.

Grant Wood is producing an art that is real, indigenous to the life of his people. He has brought the town of Cedar Rapids and the state of Iowa renown and is, in my mind, the perfect example of that situation talked about now—"the artist as a part of his civilization." Not only have the people of Cedar Rapids bought 400 of his pictures, but his advice is asked on the architecture and design of public buildings; the leading hotel is decorated by his hand.

Reginald Marsh will put into a Coney Island Beach crowd something more than the fact—there is in these people the squirm of life. In the work of Burchfield and Hopper there is more than the reporting of a mansard roof—there is in them the history of a period. Jacob Burek painted a picture of a striker being slugged by mine guards; it is one of the few propaganda pictures that has enough reality to be remembered.

The artists who are moved to paint propaganda, particularly those with Communistic leanings, should look to the realities of their subjects and at the same time become better propagandists. It would be a good thing for the John Reed Club to go en masse to a sweat shop and sketch the workers. At the Forum held last year after the social conscious art show, I heard a letter from a worker read. The workers from the sweat shop had been invited to attend and see themselves as an artist had depicted them. This one was insulted and voiced the united disapproval of the group. He said, "if this in reality is what the workers are, miserable beasts, then we are poor material out of which to build a new social order."

Cartoonists, illustrators, fashionable portrait painters are all loaded down with stock mannerisms and symbols, but none so much as the radical artist. There is a great opportunity for a new viewpoint. A little intelligent observation and a more powerful art expression would arise. It would be better propaganda too. Suppose we take the subject of a mounted cop cracking a Union Square radical over the head. The dramatic element of a man on horseback and a man on foot in combat is the best of drama. The instinctive recoil of

Originally appeared
in *Art Digest*
(September 1935): 29.

the man on foot from the trampling hoofs of the horse is good drama. Then observe the people, the open, yelling, screaming mouths. Take the worker being struck. Usually he is depicted as a flat-headed oaf, who would not be hurt much by anything, or else he appears as an emaciated wretch, for whom the cop would immediately call an ambulance. It would be better drama and better history if the type were a flesh-and-blood Union Square type.

I point out this opportunity for a new and truer approach to a very popular subject matter. I do not say there is any set manner or method of handling a subject. Some artist may come along tomorrow and, using all the old clap-trap, make something out of it—but to do it will take a fresh and vivid enthusiasm.

All good picture making depends on a design significant to the subject. I believe in subject matter. The artist ought to paint people doing things, or if he paints a portrait, to show the personality and inner meaning of the life before him. The use of life as an excuse for clever arrangements of color or other pictorial elements ends where it begins. It is well, if you would make a dramatic design, to think of the life before you. If you feel the significance of the life, the design builds itself. The feeling inherent in the life of the world cannot be ignored or trifled with for the sake of a theory.

Every sincere artist knows that there is no band wagon that goes all the way; no seeming success of the moment that will atone for the thing he knows in his heart he has not accomplished or for that thing he has left undone.

18. *Hogs Killing Rattlesnake*, 1925, watercolor on paper, Syracuse University Collection

19. *Study of a Head*, 1927, charcoal, 24½ x 18½ inches
The Elvehjem Art Center, University of Wisconsin–Madison, Board of Regents Appropriations Fund

20. *Storm over Lake Otsego*, 1929, oil on canvas, 40 x 50 inches
Museum of Fine Arts, Boston, Gift of Emily Douglass Forness

21. *Portrait, My Mother and Father*, 1929, oil on canvas, 30 x 36 inches
IBM Corporation, Armonk, New York

22. *State Fair*, 1928–1929, oil on canvas, 72 x 92 inches, Kennedy Galleries, Inc.

23. *The Ne'er Do Well*, 1929, oil on canvas, 20 x 26 inches, Whitney Museum of American Art, New York

24. *The Stockman*, 1929, oil on canvas, 52 x 40 inches, Whitney Museum of American Art, New York

25. *The Gospel Train*, 1929, oil on canvas, 40 x 52 inches, Syracuse University Collection

26. *Stallion and Jack*, 1930, watercolor, 22¼ x 27 inches, William Rockhill Nelson Gallery
of Art and Atkins Museum of Fine Arts, Gift of Mr. Paul Gardner through the Friends of Art

27. *Horses Running Before a Storm*, 1930, ink and watercolor, 14 x 19⅞ inches
Whitney Museum of American Art, New York

28. *The Manhunt*, 1931, oil on canvas, 30 x 40¼ inches, Kennedy Galleries, Inc.

29. *Spring Shower: Western Kansas Landscape*, 1931, oil on canvas, 29⅞ x 43⅞ inches
The Metropolitan Museum of Art, Arthur H. Hearn Fund, 1932

30. *The Flying Cadonas*, 1932, tempera and oil on composition board, 36 x 30 inches
Whitney Museum of American Art, New York

31. *Circus Elephants*, 1932, oil on canvas, 24¼ x 36⅛ inches
National Gallery of Art, Gift of Adm. Neill Phillips in Memory of Grace Hendrick Phillips, 1976

32. *The Hen and Hawk*, 1934, oil on canvas, 19½ x 25¼ inches
Brooks Memorial Art Gallery, Bequest of Mrs. C. M. Gooch

33. *The Line Storm*, 1934, oil and tempera on canvas, dimensions unavailable, collection unknown

34. *Sanctuary*, 1935, oil on board, 24⅓ x 30½ inches
Pennsylvania Academy of the Fine Arts, Collections Fund Purchase

35. *The Mississippi*, 1935, tempera on canvas, 36 x 47½ inches, St. Louis Art Museum

36. *Ajax*, 1936, oil on canvas, 36¼ x 48¾ inches, Kennedy Galleries, Inc.

37. *At the Circus*, 1936, oil on canvas, 21 x 30½ inches, Kennedy Galleries, Inc.

38. *The Belgian Stallion*, 1938 oil on panel, 30 x 25 inches
National Academy of Design, Gift of the Artist

39. *Parade to War: Allegory*, 1939, oil on canvas, 40½ x 56 inches, Kennedy Galleries, Inc.

40. *The Fugitive*, 1933–1940, oil on canvas, 38 x 36 inches, Kennedy Galleries, Inc.

41. *Wisconsin Still Life*, 1940, oil on panel, 44½ x 30 inches, Kennedy Galleries, Inc.

42. *Leaving the Farm for Army Training Camp*, 1941, tempera, 15 x 42 inches
The New Britain Museum of American Art

43. *Madison, Wisconsin, Landscape*, 1941, oil and tempera on canvas, 87 x 96 inches
First Wisconsin National Bank of Madison

44. *Wisconsin Farm Landscape*, 1941, oil and tempera on canvas, 87 x 96 inches
First Wisconsin National Bank of Madison

45. *Self-Portrait*, 1942, oil on board, dimensions not available, Kennedy Galleries, Inc.

46. *Cuba*, 1946, oil on canvas, 25½ x 33 inches, Kennedy Galleries, Inc.

47. *The Three Wise Men*, 1927, lithograph, 8¼ x 6⅛ inches (C-1)*
Syracuse University

48. *Coyotes Stealing a Pig*, 1927, lithograph, 10⅛ x 15⅛ inches (C-2)
Photograph Courtesy Davenport Art Gallery

49. *Coyotes Stealing a Pig*, 1927, lithograph, 10 x 15 inches (C-3)

50. *Wild Bill Cody*, 1927, lithograph, 17¼ x 12⅛ inches (C-4)

51. *Plainsmen and Indians*, 1927–1928, lithograph, 14 x 17½ inches (C-5)
Photograph Courtesy Davenport Art Gallery

52. *Family Migrates*, 1929, lithograph, 4½ x 6⅝ inches (C-6)
Photograph Courtesy Davenport Art Gallery

53. *Wheat Ranch Kansas*, ca. 1929, lithograph, 3¼ x 4¾ inches (C-7)

54. *Danbury Fair*, 1930, lithograph, 13 x 9¾ inches (C-8)

55. *Holy Rollers*, 1930, lithograph, 9 x 12⅞ inches (C-9)

56. *Horses Running Before the Storm*, 1930, lithograph, 9½ x 13 inches (C-10)

57. *The Storm*, 1930, lithograph, 4⅝ x 6⅝ inches (C-11)

58. *Kansas Wheat Ranch*, 1930, lithograph, 9½ x 13⅝ inches (C-12)
Photograph Courtesy Davenport Art Gallery

59. *Hounds and Coyote*, 1931, lithograph, 10 x 14 inches (C-13)

60. *Ajax*, 1931, lithograph, 9¾ x 13⅝ inches (C-14)

61. *Baptism in Big Stranger Creek*, 1932, lithograph, 9⅞ x 13⅝ inches (C-15)

62. *The Tornado*, 1932, lithograph, 10 x 14 inches (C-16)

63. *To the Train*, 1932, lithograph, 9⅞ x 13⅞ inches (C-17)

64. *Mississippi Noah*, 1932, lithograph, 9¾ x 13⅝ inches (C-18)
Photograph Courtesy Davenport Art Gallery

65. *The Missed Leap*, 1932, lithograph, 16⅞ x 9¾ inches (C-19)

66. *The Flying Cadonas*, 1933, lithograph, 15⅞ x 9⅞ inches (C-20)

67. *Storm over Stone City*, 1935, lithograph, 10⅝ x 17⅛ inches (C-21)

68. *The Oak Tree*, 1934, lithograph, 13¾ x 10 inches (C-22)

69. *The Oak Tree*, 1934, wash on paper, 12⅛ x 11 inches (C-22)

70. *Performing Tiger*, 1934, lithograph, 10½ x 14 inches (C-23)
Photograph Courtesy Davenport Art Gallery

71. *Manhunt*, 1934, lithograph, 9¾ x 12⅞ inches (C-24)

72. *Mississippi Noah*, ca. 1934, lithograph, 9⅞ x 13¾ inches (C-25)

73. *The Cornfield*, 1935, lithograph, 12⅞ x 9½ inches (C-26)

74. *The Fugitive*, 1935, lithograph, 12⅞ x 9⅜ inches (C-27)

75. *The Fugitive*, 1935, charcoal on paper, 14¾ x 11½ inches (C-27)

76. *The Line Storm*, 1935, lithograph, 9¾ x 13⅞ inches (C-28)

77. *Elephants*, 1936, lithograph, 9 x 12⅝ inches (C-29)

78. *Football Game*, 1938, lithograph, 9⅞ x 13⅞ inches (C-30)
Photograph Courtesy Davenport Art Gallery

79. *Football Game*, 1938, pencil on paper, 10 x 14 inches (C-30)

80. *End Run*, 1938, lithograph, 10 x 13¾ inches (C-31)

81. *Prize Stallions*, 1938, lithograph, 12¾ x 8¾ inches (C-32)

82. *Self*, 1939, lithograph, 11 x 9¼ inches (C-33)
Photograph Courtesy Davenport Art Gallery

83. *Self-Portrait*, 1939, lithograph, 12¾ x 9⅝ inches (C-34)

84. *John Brown*, 1939, lithograph, 14¾ x 10⅞ inches (C-35)

85. *Summer Afternoon*, 1939, lithograph, 10 x 13⅞ inches (C-36)
Photograph Courtesy Davenport Art Gallery

86. *Our Good Earth*, 1940–1941, lithograph, 12¾ x 10⅛ inches (C-37)

87. *Our Good Earth*, 1940–1941, lithograph, 12¾ x 10⅛ inches (C-38)

88. *Stallion and Jack Fighting*, 1943, lithograph, 11¾ x 15⅜ inches (C-39)

89. *Stallion and Jack Fighting*, 1943, crayon on paper, 16½ x 21½ inches (C-39)

90. *Sanctuary*, 1944, lithograph, 9 x 11⅞ inches (C-40)

91. *Sanctuary*, 1944, pencil on paper, 12 x 16 inches (C-40)

92. *Sanctuary*, 1944, lithograph, 11¾ x 15¾ inches (C-41)

93. *Sanctuary*, 1944, pencil on paper, 12¼ x 16 inches (C-41)

94. *The Plainsman*, 1945, lithograph, 15¾ x 9⅝ inches (C-42)

95. *Valley of the Wisconsin*, 1945, lithograph, 11¾ x 15⅜ inches (C-43)

96. *Valley of the Wisconsin*, 1945, pencil on paper, 10¼ x 14 inches (C-43)

Graphics of John Steuart Curry: A Catalogue Raisonné

C–1. *The Three Wise Men*, 1927 (Figure 47)
Lithograph, 8¼ x 6⅛ inches (Cole No. 1)
Edition of 42. Unsigned on stone
Collections: Dav, SU
Note: This print was completed at the Art Students' League under Charles Wheeler Locke (b. 1877). The location of preliminary drawings or sketches is unknown.

C–2. *Coyotes Stealing a Pig*, 1927 (Figure 48)
Lithograph, 10⅛ x 15⅛ inches (Cole No. 2)
Edition of 16. First stone. Signed on stone, lower left:
    "J. Curry"
"Collection: Dav
Note: This print was completed at the Art Students' League under Charles Wheeler Locke (b. 1877). The location of preliminary drawings or sketches is unknown. This print is similar in theme to a series of works including *Hogs Killing a Rattlesnake* (Figure 18), *The Hen and Hawk* (Figure 32), *Hounds and Coyote* (Figure 60), and *Stallion and Jack Fighting* (Figure 86).

C–3. *Coyotes Stealing a Pig*, 1927 (Figure 49)
Lithograph, 10 x 15 inches (Cole No. 3)
Edition of 50. Second stone. Signed on stone, lower right:
    "J. Curry"
Collections: Dav, MFAB
Note: This print was completed at the Art Students' League under Charles Wheeler Locke (b. 1877). The location of preliminary drawings or sketches is unknown. This print is similar in theme to a series of works including *Hogs Killing a Rattlesnake* (Figure 18), *The Hen and Hawk* (Figure 32), *Hounds and Coyote* (Figure 60), and *Stallion and Jack Fighting* (Figure 86).

C–4. *Wild Bill Cody*, 1927 (Figure 50)
Alternate Title: *Frontiersman*
Lithograph, 17¼ x 12⅛ inches (Cole No. 4)
Edition of 2. Signed on stone, lower left: "Curry"
Collections: Dav, private collection
Note: This print was completed at the Art Students' League under Charles Wheeler Locke (b. 1877). The location of preliminary drawings or sketches is unknown. This print is similar in theme to a 1925 mural design, *Plainsmen, Pioneers, Surveyors* (Schmeckebier, p. 275, pl. 288a), done as an experiment by Curry to reveal "what . . . [he] thought a genuinely American mural art should be." While only two copies of this lithograph were made, the other, dated 1928, appears to be inferior. The stirrup on Wild Bill's foot does not appear on the second copy.

C–5. *Plainsmen and Indians*, 1927–1928 (Figure 51)
Alternate Title: *The Trapper*
Lithograph, 14 x 17½ inches (Cole No. 5)
Edition unknown, proofs only. Signed on stone, lower right:
    "J. S. Curry"
Collections: Dav (signed by artist's widow)
Note: This print was completed at the Art Students' League under Charles Wheeler Locke (b. 1877). The location of preliminary drawings or sketches is unknown. This print is similar in theme to a 1925 mural design, *Plainsmen, Pioneers, Surveyors* (Schmeckebier, p. 275, pl. 288a), done as an experiment by Curry to reveal "what . . . [he] thought a genuinely American mural art should be."

C–6. *Family Migrates*, 1929 (Figure 52)
Alternate Title: *Flight into Egypt, The Ne'er Do Well*
Lithograph, 4½ x 6⅝ inches (Cole No. 6)
Edition of 100. Signed on stone, lower left: "J.S.C."
Collection: Dav
Note: This print is similar in subject to *The Ne'er Do Well* (Figure 23). Preliminary sketches were begun in the summer of 1929 and show an actual scene viewed from the porch of his father's house in Dunavant, Kansas. Represented is a migratory farm family moving from the drought and foreclosures in Oklahoma and Arkansas to the profitable countryside of Kansas and Nebraska (Schmeckebier, pp. 125–26, pls. 76–77). It is also related to a painting in oil on paper in the collection of Kennedy Galleries, Inc. (*John Brown-Mellora in Cart*, 22 x 38½ inches). *Family Migrates* is the contemporary title as recorded in the *Handbook of the American Artists Group*, New York, volume 2, 1936, no. 1555, p. 23.

C–7. *Wheat Ranch Kansas*, ca. 1929 (Figure 53)
Lithograph, 3¼ x 4¾ inches (Cole No. 7)
Edition of 100. Unsigned on stone
Collection: Dav
Note: This print is similar in theme to a series of drawings dated 1930 of the Heart Ranch, Barber County, Kansas (Schmeckebier, p. 135, pl. 85). Many of these preliminary drawings are in the collection of Kennedy Galleries, Inc.

C–8. *Danbury Fair*, 1930 (Figure 54)
Lithograph, 13 x 9¾ inches (Cole No. 8)
Edition of 25. Signed on stone, lower right, "ʟ. Curry ƐO"
Collections: Dav, MMA, PMA, Wichita
Note: The location of preliminary drawings or sketches is unknown. This print is similar in subject to a painting in oil on canvas dated 1929 and titled *State Fair* in the collection of Kennedy Galleries, Inc. Painted in Westport, Connecticut, *State Fair* was conceived in mural terms, "Framed by elaborate garlands of fruit and grain, and painted in brilliant colors that have the cool luminosity of a fresco technique" (Schmeckebier, p. 206, pl. 181).

C–9. *Holy Rollers*, 1930 (Figure 55)
Alternate Title: *The Gospel Train, St. Joseph, Mo.*
Lithograph, 9 x 12⅞ inches (Cole No. 9)
Edition of 25. Signed on stone, lower left: "ʟ. Curry ƐO"
Collections: Dav, PMA, SU
Note: The location of preliminary drawings or sketches is unknown; however, Schmeckebier (p. 100) does indicate that at least two pages of sketches do exist. This print is similar in subject to a painting, *The Gospel Train* (Figure 25).

C–10. *Horses Running Before the Storm*, 1930 (Figure 56)
Lithograph, 9½ x 13 inches (Cole No. 10)
Edition unknown, about 25. Signed on stone, lower left: "J. Curry 30"
Collections: CMA, Dav, NYPL, PMA, WM
Note: This print is similar to the watercolor, Figure 27. Also, the motif

of the excited horses is seen in the background pasture of the lithograph and painting of *The Tornado* (Figure 5 and Schmeckebier, pp. 113–14, pl. 61).

C–11. *The Storm*, 1930 (Figure 57)
Lithograph, 4⅝ x 6⅝ inches (Cole No. 11)

Edition of 400. Unsigned on stone
Collection: Dav
Note: This print is similar to the painting *Storm over Lake Otsego* (Figure 20). It is based on sketches made in the Lake Otsego region near Cooperstown, New York (Schmeckebier, p. 113, pl. 60).

C–12. *Kansas Wheat Ranch*, 1930 (Figure 58)
Lithograph, 9½ x 13⅝ inches
Edition of 25. Signed on stone, lower left: "J. S. Curry"
Collections: CMA, Dav, Swarthmore
Note: This print is similar to a painting in oil on canvas dated 1930 in a private collection (Schmeckebier, p. 135, pl. 84).

C–13. *Hounds and Coyote*, 1931 (Figure 59)
Lithograph, 10 x 14 inches (Cole No. 12)
Edition of 25. Signed on stone, lower left: "John S. Curry 31"
Collections: Dav, PMA
Note: This print is similar to a series of preliminary sketches (Schmeckebier, pp. 198–99, pls. 169–71). One of Curry's favorite lithographs, this print explores the compositional idea of fierce action in space.

C–14. *Ajax*, 1931 (Figure 60)
Lithograph, 9¾ x 13⅝ inches (Cole No. 14)
Edition of 25. Signed on stone, lower right: "l. Curry"
Collections: Dav, Wichita
Note: This print is similar in subject to a painting, *Ajax* (Figure 36). As verified by Schmeckebier (p. 186), the lithograph *Ajax* was completed in 1931 but accidentally dated 1932 for Thomas Craven's *Treasury of American Prints*. Described as "galvanic" by Tom Benton, *Ajax* dates to sketches of grazing Herefords made during the summer of 1930. The landscape is similar to that surrounding the Heart Ranch, Barber County, Kansas.

C–15. *Baptism in Big Stranger Creek*, 1932 (Figure 61)
Lithograph, 9⅞ x 13⅝ inches (Cole No. 13)
Edition of 25. Signed on stone, lower right: "J.C."
Collections: Dav, PMA
Note: The location of preliminary sketches or drawings is unknown. As indicated by Schmeckebier (p. 104), the scene was actually observed and not composed from memory as was *Baptism in Kansas* (Figure 2).

C–16. *The Tornado*, 1932 (Figure 62)
Lithograph, 10 x 14 inches (Cole No. 15)
Edition of 25. Signed on stone, lower right: "J. Curry"
Collections: Bowdoin, Dav, MMA, Okl, WM
Note: This print is similar to a painting in oil on canvas dated 1929 in the collection of the Hackley Art Gallery, Muskegon, Michigan. For a full discussion of the painting, see Schmeckebier, pp. 111–13.

C–17. *To the Train*, 1932 (Figure 63)
Lithograph, 9⅞ x 13⅞ inches (Cole No. 16)
Edition of 30. Signed on stone, lower left: "John S. Curry"
Collections: Bklyn, Dav, MMA, SU, Wichita
Note: This print is similar in subject to a drawing in the collection of Kennedy Galleries, Inc.

C–18. *Mississippi Noah*, 1932 (Figure 64)
Lithograph, 9¾ x 13⅝ inches (Cole No. 17)
One proof only, stone destroyed. Signed on stone, lower right: "JSC"
Collection: Dav
Note: This print is similar in subject to a painting, *The Mississippi* (Figure 35). Derived from a series of sketches, this print relates a flood in the Kaw River Valley near Lawrence, Kansas, observed while Curry was there in 1929.

C–19. *The Missed Leap*, 1932 (Figure 65)
Lithograph, 16⅞ x 9¾ inches (Cole No. 23)
Edition of 250. Signed on stone, lower left: "Curry"
Collections: Amherst, Col, Dav, FAMSF, MFAB, N–A, NCFA, Princeton, SL, WAM, Wichita
Note: This print is similar to the drawing in black crayon and watercolor dated 1932 and titled *Aerialist's Fall* (Schmeckebier, p. 228, pl. 219). This print was distributed to the public in a new edition in 1934 by Associated American Artists. Initial 100 impressions are numbered. Cole indicates an additional edition of 150 was printed and unnumbered. Unsigned proofs also exist.

C–20. *The Flying Cadonas*, 1933 (Figure 66)
Lithograph, 15⅞ x 9⅞ inches (Cole No. 18)
Edition of 50. Signed on stone, lower left: "John S. Curry"
Collections: Dav, MMA
Note: This print is similar to a painting, *The Flying Cadonas* (Figure 30). It depicts Alfredo Cadona in a triple somersault as he is hurled through the air to the grip of his brother Lala. Several related sketches in sepia, red chalk, and watercolor do exist in the collection of Kennedy Galleries, Inc. (Schmeckebier, pp. 220–22, pls. 200–207).

C–21. *Storm over Stone City*, 1935 (Figure 67)
Lithograph, 10⅝ x 17⅛ inches (Cole No. 19)
Edition of 15. Signed on stone, lower left: "Curry"
Collections: Dav, MMA
Note: The location of preliminary sketches or drawings is unknown. This print was done at the Stone City Art Colony in July 1933, during a visit to Grant Wood.

C–22. *The Oak Tree*, 1934 (Figure 68)
Alternate Title: *Oak Tree: Summer*
Lithograph, 13¾ x 10 inches (Cole No. 20)
Edition of 50. Signed on stone, lower left: "John S. Curry"
Collections: Dav, SFMA, UNC
Note: This print is similar to a painting dated 1935 titled *The Oak Tree: Summer* (collection unknown), exhibited in the 110th Annual Exhibition of the National Academy of Design. This drawing is quite similar in subject to Figure 69, in the collection of Kennedy Galleries, Inc.

C–23. *Performing Tiger*, 1934 (Figure 70)
Lithograph, 10½ x 14 inches (Cole No. 21)
Edition of 25. Signed on stone, lower right: "J. S. Curry"
Collection: Dav
Note: This print is similar to a series of drawings in sepia and black crayon dated 1932 and titled *Clyde Beatty and Animal Act* (Schmeckebier, pp. 230–33, pls. 225–33). It is also related to a painting in oil on canvas (20½ x 30½ inches) dated 1932 and titled *Clyde Beatty* in the collection of Kennedy Galleries, Inc.

C–24. *Manhunt*, 1934 (Figure 71)
Lithograph, 9¾ x 12⅞ inches (Cole No. 22)

Edition of 100 or less. Signed on stone, lower left: "J. Curry"; published by Contemporary Print Group, New York; distributed by Raymond and Raymond, Inc., in the portfolio *The American Scene, Series 2*.
Collections: Dav, FAMSF, MOMA, NYPL, Oberlin, UM, Wichita, WM
Note: Originally intended to be an edition of 300, the portfolio was not successful and probably less than 100 impressions were printed. This print is similar to the oil painting, *Manhunt* (Figure 28).

C–25. *Mississippi Noah*, ca. 1934 (Figure 72)
Lithograph, 9⅞ x 13¾ inches (Cole No. 24)

Edition of 35. Signed on stone, lower left: "J. Curry"
Collections: Dav, MMA, NYPL, SL, WM
Note: This print is similar in subject to a painting, *The Mississippi* (Figure 35). Derived from a series of sketches, this print related a flood in the Kaw River Valley near Lawrence, Kansas, observed while Curry was there in 1929. The St. Louis Art Museum impression is clearly dated 1934 and is noted "35 prints." It was acquired from Walker Galleries at the same time the museum purchased the painting.

C–26. *The Cornfield*, 1935 (Figure 73)
Lithograph, 12⅞ x 9½ inches (Cole No. 25)
Edition of 25. Signed on stone, lower left: "JSC"
Collections: Dav, MFAB, UNC
Note: This print is similar in subject to a painting, *Kansas Cornfield* (Figure 1). It is also related to a sketchbook dated 1933 full of corn studies (Schmeckebier, pp. 157–58, pls. 108–9).

C–27. *The Fugitive*, 1935 (Figure 74)
Lithograph, 12⅞ x 9⅜ inches (Cole No. 26)
Edition of 25. Signed on stone, lower left: "JSC"
Collections: Dav, Elv, MFAB, NCFA, NYPL
Note: This print is similar in subject to a painting, *The Fugitive* (Figure 40). It is also very similar to the drawing, Figure 75, in the collection of Kennedy Galleries, Inc.

C–28. *The Line Storm*, 1935 (Figure 76)
Lithograph, 9¾ x 13⅞ inches (Cole No. 27)
Edition of 25. Signed on stone, lower left: "JSC"
Collections: Dav, MFAB, NCFA, PMA
Note: Published as second state, it is doubtful that the overall edition exceeded 25. This print is similar in subject to a painting, *The Line Storm* (Figure 33).

C–29. *Elephants*, 1936 (Figure 77)
Alternate Title: *Circus Elephants*
Lithograph, 9 x 12⅝ inches (Cole No. 28)
Edition of 250. Signed on stone, lower right: "JSC"; published and distributed by Associated American Artists, New York.
Collections: Col, Dav, FAMSF, Minn, NCFA, RM, UN
Note: This print is similar in subject to a painting in oil on canvas dated 1932 in the collection of the National Gallery of Art (Schmeckebier, pl. 237). Curry described the circumstances in which he sketched the elephants in Schmeckebier, p. 210.

C–30. *Football Game*, 1938 (Figure 78)
Alternate Title: *Off Tackle*
Lithograph, 9⅞ x 13⅞ inches (Cole No. 29)
Edition unknown, proofs only. Signed on stone, lower left:
    "JSC 38"
Collection: Dav
Note: This print is similar in subject to a series of black crayon draw-ings of the University of Wisconsin–Madison football team scrimmages and games. It is also very similar to the drawing, Figure 79, in the collection of Kennedy Galleries, Inc.

C–31. *End Run*, 1938 (Figure 80)
Lithograph, 10 x 13¾ inches (Cole No. 30)
Edition unknown, proofs only. Signed on stone, lower left:
    "JSC 38"
Collection: Dav
Note: The location of preliminary drawings and sketches is unknown. This print is similar in subject to a series of black crayon sketches of an end run dated 1938 and two oil sketches of an end run dated 1938 (Schmeckebier, pp. 245–47, pls. 259–63).

C–32. *Prize Stallions*, 1938 (Figure 81)
Lithograph, 12¾ x 8¾ inches (Cole No. 31)
Edition of 250. Signed on stone, lower left: "JSC 38"; published and distributed by Associated American Artists, New York.
Collections: Amherst, BMA, BMAG, Dav, FAMSF, Kal, MFAB, NYPL,
    Oberlin, UN, WM
Note: According to Schmeckebier (p. 292), the composition originated from a red chalk drawing that Curry made for the cover of the *Wisconsin Country Magazine*, published by University of Wisconsin agriculture students. The location of preliminary drawings and sketches is unknown. This print is similar in subject to a painting, *The Belgian Stallion* (Figure 38). It is also a logical compositional development from the painting in oil and tempera on panel (24½ x 30½ inches) dated 1937 in the collection of the New Britain Museum of American Art. This was the first painting completed after Curry accepted his position of artist in residence at the University of Wisconsin.

C–33. *Self*, 1939 (Figure 82)
Lithograph, 11 x 9¼ inches (Cole No. 32)
One proof only. Signed on stone, lower right: "JSC 39"
Collection: Dav
Note: The location of preliminary drawings and sketches is unknown. This print is related to a series of self-portraits that were begun in 1925 and continued through the 1940s. It is also similar to a lithograph, *Self-Portrait* (Figure 83).

C–34. *Self-Portrait*, 1939 (Figure 83)
Alternate Title: *Self*
Lithograph, 12¾ x 9⅝ inches (Cole No. 33)
No edition, proofs only. Signed on stone, lower left: "JSC 39"
Collections: Dav, LC
Note: The location of preliminary drawings and sketches is unknown. Portrayed as a hunter, according to Schmeckebier (p. 141), Curry is in the cornfields to the west of his small Madison farm purchased that year.

C–35. *John Brown*, 1939 (Figure 84)
Lithograph, 14¾ x 10⅞ inches (Cole No. 34)
Edition of 250. Signed on stone, lower right: "JSC 39"; published and distributed by Associated American Artists, New York, in 1940.
Collections: BMAG, BPL, CAM, CMA, Col, DIA, FAMSF, Fogg, HMA,
    MFAB, N–A, Okl, PMA, UI, Yale
Note: This print is similar to the painting, *John Brown* (Figure 7). It is also similar to the figure of John Brown in the mural *The Tragic Prelude* (138 x 372 inches) on the north wall of the Kansas State Capitol, Topeka.

C–36. *Summer Afternoon*, 1939 (Figure 85)
Lithograph, 10 x 13⅞ inches (Cole No. 35)
Edition of 250. Signed on stone, lower left: "JSC"; published and distributed by Associated American Artists, New York.
Collections: Bklyn, BMAG, Col, Cornell, Dav, FAMSF
Note: The location of preliminary drawings and sketches is unknown. The date 1939 is derived from the signed and dated impression in the collection of the Fine Arts Museum of San Francisco (Achenbach Foundation). The lithograph is similar to a transfer drawing in the collection of Kennedy Galleries, Inc.

C–37. *Our Good Earth*, 1940–1941 (Figure 86)
Lithograph, 12¾ x 10⅛ inches
No edition, proofs only. Signed on stone, lower left: "JSC"
Collection: Dav
Note: The location of preliminary drawings and sketches is unknown. This print is similar in theme to the 1938 mural (oil and tempera on canvas, 110 x 236 inches) *The Homestead* in the Department of the Interior, Washington, D.C.

C–38. *Our Good Earth*, 1940–1941 (Figure 87)
Lithograph, 12¾ x 10⅛ inches (Cole No. 36)
Edition of 250. Signed on stone, lower right: "JSC"; published and distributed by Associated American Artists, New York, in 1942.
Collections: BMAG, Fogg, Kal, LC, Minn, NCFA
Note: The location of preliminary drawings and sketches is unknown. A measure of uncertainty exists about the date of this lithograph. In a catalogue accompanying a September 5–October 15, 1946, exhibition of Curry's work at the Milwaukee Art Center, *Our Good Earth* was dated 1940–1941 (No. 170, lent by Associated American Artists, New York). Also, the impression in the Library of Congress collection is dated 1938. As such, it is quite possible that the composition was developed by Curry over a series of years, until the design was satisfactory.

C–39. *Stallion and Jack Fighting*, 1943 (Figure 88)
Lithograph, 11¾ x 15⅜ inches (Cole No. 37)
Edition of 250. Signed on stone, lower left: "JSC 43"; published and distributed by Associated American Artists, New York.
Collections: Amherst, BMAG, CMA, Col, Dart, Dav, FAMSF, Fogg, MFAB, MMA, Wichita
Note: This print is similar in subject to a painting in oil on canvas dated 1930 (collection unknown, Schmeckebier, pp. 197–98, pl. 165). It is also similar to a watercolor study (Figure 26) in the collection of the Nelson Gallery–Atkins Museum, Kansas City. It is also very similar to a drawing, Figure 89, in the collection of Kennedy Galleries, Inc.

C–40. *Sanctuary*, 1944 (Figure 90)
Alternate Title: *Flood Relief*
Lithograph, 9 x 11⅞ inches (Cole No. 39)
Edition unknown, proofs only. Signed on stone, lower left: "JSC"
Collection: Dav
Note: This print is similar to a watercolor drawing of 1933 (Schmeckebier, p. 119, pl. 72) and to a painting, *Sanctuary* (Figure 34). It is based on a series of drawings of the floods in the Kaw River Valley near Lawrence, Kansas, observed by Curry in 1929. As previously indicated, another related work of the same theme is *The Mississippi* (Figure 35), or *Mississippi Noah* (Figure 72). It is also very similar to a drawing, Figure 91, in the collection of Kennedy Galleries, Inc.

C–41. *Sanctuary*, 1944 (Figure 92)
Alternate Title: *Flood Relief*
Lithograph, 11¾ x 15¾ inches (Cole No. 38)
Edition of 250. Signed on stone, lower right: "JSC 44"; published and distributed by Associated American Artists, New York.
Collections: BMAG, BPL, Col, Dart, Dav, FAMSF, IMA, UI, WAM, Wichita
Note: This print is similar to a watercolor drawing of 1933 (Schmeckebier, p. 119, pl. 72) and to a painting, *Sanctuary* (Figure 34). It is based on a series of drawings of the floods in the Kaw River Valley near Lawrence, Kansas, observed by Curry in 1929. As previously indicated, another related work of the same theme is *The Mississippi* (Figure 35), or *Mississippi Noah* (Figure 72). It is also very similar to a drawing, Figure 93, in the collection of Kennedy Galleries, Inc.

C–42. *The Plainsman*, 1945 (Figure 94)
Lithograph, 15¾ x 9⅝ inches (Cole No. 40)
Edition of 250. Signed on stone, lower right: "JSC 45"; published and distributed by Associated American Artists, New York.
Collections: BMAG, Dart, Dav, FAMSF, IMA, MFAB, MMA, NCFA, UN
Note: This print is similar to the figure of the plainsman in the 1938 mural *The Tragic Prelude* in the Kansas State Capitol, Topeka. It is also similar to a preliminary study in oil on board (30¼ x 20 inches) dated ca. 1940 in the collection of Kennedy Galleries, Inc.

C–43. *Valley of the Wisconsin*, 1945 (Figure 95)
Lithograph, 11¾ x 15⅜ inches (Cole No. 41)
Edition of 250. Signed on stone, lower right: "JSC 45"; published and distributed by Associated American Artists, New York.
Collections: Dav, Fogg, MFAB, MMA, NCFA
Note: The location of preliminary sketches and drawings is unknown. This print is similar to the 1941 mural in oil and tempera on canvas depicting Wisconsin scenes in the lobby of the First Wisconsin National Bank of Madison. It is also very similar to a drawing, Figure 96, in the collection of Kennedy Galleries, Inc.

Chronology: John Steuart Curry

1897 Born 14 November on a farm near Dunavant, Kansas, the eldest of five children, of Scotch Covenanter parents, Smith Curry (dates unknown) and Margaret Steuart Curry (dates unknown). His parents' families originally migrated from the Chester district of South Carolina.

1909 Received first art lessons from Mrs. Alice Worwick in nearby Oskaloosa, Kansas.

1913–1916 Attended high school in Winchester. Expressed earliest interest in athletics, especially football and track.

1916 Moved to Kansas City in the summer and entered the Art Institute. Remained for only a month, then went to work for the Missouri Pacific Railroad. Moved to Chicago in October and entered the School of the Art Institute of Chicago. Studied with Edward J. Timmons and John W. Norton.

1918 Completed studies at Art Institute of Chicago, March. Moved to Beaver Falls, Pennsylvania, and entered Geneva College.

1919 Left Geneva College and moved to Leonia, New Jersey, where he began serious work as a free-lance illustrator, largely under the influence of Harvey Dunn (1884–1952).

1921–1926 Contributed illustrations to Western stories published in *Boy's Life, St. Nicholas, Country Gentleman, Saturday Evening Post*, and other Curtis publications.

1923 Married Clara Derrick (?–1932) and lived in Greenwich Village, New York City. Spent summer in a rented cabin in the old James Fenimore Cooper estate on Lake Otsego, near Cooperstown, New York.

1924 Moved to Westport, Connecticut, and bought a studio at Otter Ponds. Continued work as an illustrator; however, his designs were becoming increasingly similar to finished paintings.

1925 Exhibited: *The Fence Builders* (1922) at the National Academy of Design, 15 November–7 December. Completed the watercolor *Hogs Killing a Rattlesnake* (Figure 18), subsequently purchased by the etcher-sculptor Harry Wickey (1892–1968).

1926 Financed by Seward Prosser, Curry traveled to Paris for the first time, arriving in October. Lived in the rue Daguerre studio of the American sculptor, Hunt Dietrich, and studied with the Russian academician Basil Schoukhaieff (1877–?).

1927 Exhibited result of his studies with Schoukhaieff at the Dronat Galleries on the rue de Rennes in May. Drawings (*Study of a Head*, Figure 19) praised by Georges Bal of the *Paris Herald-Tribune*. Returned to Westport in June. Studied lithography at the Art Students' League in New York with Charles Wheeler Locke (b. 1877), November–December 1927 to January 1928. Produced earliest lithographs.

1928 Continued painting in his Westport studio. By summer, completed *Baptism in Kansas* (Figure 2); subsequently exhibited in the 11th Biennial Exhibition of Contemporary American Oil Paintings at the Corcoran Gallery, 28 October–9 December. Received first public recognition as an important American artist.

1929 Visited his parents on the farm at Dunavant, Kansas, and remained for six weeks. Sketched farm scenes extensively and by fall completed the following paintings: *The Tornado* (Figure 5), *Storm over Lake Otsego* (Figure 20), *Portrait, My Father and Mother* (Figure 21).

1930 One-man exhibit held at the Whitney Studio Galleries (dates unknown); and the Ferargil Gallery, December. Praised by New York critics, his works began to sell well. Whitney Museum purchased *Baptism in Kansas, The Stockman* (Figure 24), *Ne'er Do Well* (Figure 23), and several watercolors.

1931 Two one-man exhibits held at Ferargil Gallery, March and 12–26 October.

1932 Death of Curry's first wife, Clara Derrick Curry, June. *Spring Shower: Western Kansas Landscape* (Figure 29) purchased by Metropolitan Museum of Art. Accompanied Ringling Brothers Barnum and Bailey Circus on its spring tour through New England, resulting in extensive paintings and sketches of circus life. Began to teach at Cooper Union (1932–1934) and at the Art Students' League (1932–1936).

1933 Met artist Grant Wood at the Stone City, Iowa, Art Colony, July. Awarded second prize for *The Tornado* at 31st Annual International Exhibition of Paintings of the Carnegie Institute, Pittsburgh, 19 October–10 December. Exhibited circus paintings at Ferargil Gallery, 3–16 April.

1934 Married Kathleen Gould. Painted under local sponsorship two fresco murals (8 × 13 feet each) for the auditorium of Westport High School, Connecticut. Murals entitled *Tragedy* (Schmeckebier, pl. 294) and *Comedy* (Schmeckebier, pl. 295).

1935–1936 Sponsored by Public Works of Art Project, Curry painted two oil-on-canvas murals (dimensions unavailable) for Norwalk High School, Connecticut. Murals entitled *Ancient Industry* (Schmeckebier, pl. 292) and *Modern Hat Industry* (Schmeckebier, pl. 293). Exhibited works at Ferargil Gallery, 21 January–4 February.

1936 Appointed artist-in-residence at the College of Agriculture of the University of Wisconsin–Madison. Began Department of Justice murals in Westport.

1936–1937 Completed two oil and tempera on canvas (102 × 246 inches) murals for the Department of Justice Building, Washington, D.C. Murals entitled *Westward Migration* and *Justice Defeating Mob Violence*.

1937 Presented preliminary oil sketches for approval to the Kansas State Capitol Murals Commission Committee.

1938 Traveled to Europe, completed two oil and tempera on canvas (110 × 236 inches) murals for the Department of the Interior Building, Washington, D.C. Murals entitled *The Homestead* and *The Oklahoma Land Rush* (Figure 6).

1938–1940 Developed and completed series of oil and tempera on canvas murals for the east and west corridors of the state capitol building, Topeka, Kansas. Murals entitled: *Tragic Prelude* on the east (138 × 264 inches) and north (138 × 372 inches) walls of the east corridor; and *Kansas Pastoral* on the south (128 × 312 inches) and west (138 × 264 inches) of the west corridor off the rotunda. The rotunda panels were never executed (Schmeckebier, p. 325, pl. 321).

1939 One-man exhibit of drawings and paintings at Lakeside Press Galleries, Chicago, 1 March–28 April.

1940 *Hoover and the Flood* commissioned by Life, Inc., in the spring as part of a series of paintings on recent American history. Reproduced in the 6 May issue of *Life*, it is based on Hoover's service as relief organizer during the disastrous Mississippi flood of 1927. Provided illustrations to James Fenimore Cooper's *The Prairie* published by the Limited Editions Club.

1940–1941 Developed and completed a series of oil and tempera on canvas murals for the new biochemistry building in the College of Agriculture at the University of Wisconsin–Madison. Murals entitled: *Social Benefits of Biochemical Research* (72 × 168 inches), *Benefits of Biochemical Research: Farm Stock* (108 × 55 inches), and *Corn and Tobacco* (72 × 55 inches).

1941–1942 Developed and completed a series of oil and tempera on canvas murals for the lobby of the First National Bank, Madison. Murals depict a series of characteristic views around the city—*Madison Landscape with State Capitol* (88 × 96 inches), *Corn* (40 × 29 inches), *Wisconsin Farm Landscape* (87 × 96 inches), *Autumn Landscape with Pheasant and Pumpkin* (46 × 28 inches), and *Wisconsin Landscape with Grouse* (88 × 95 inches).

1941 Received gold medal at the Pennsylvania Academy of the Fine Arts. Provided illustrations to Mary O'Hara's *My Friend Flicka* published by J. B. Lippincott(New York) and featured by the Book-of-the-Month Club.

1942 Completed an oil and tempera on canvas mural for the Law School Library at the University of Wisconsin–Madison. Developed since 1936 and based on a rejected sketch for the Department of Justice, the mural is titled *Freeing of the Slaves* (122 [sides] × 228 [center] × 444 inches). *Wisconsin Landscape* (1940) distinguished by critics at the "Artists for Victory" exhibition at the Metropolitan Museum of Art; subsequently purchased by the same institution. Provided illustrations to *The Writings of Lincoln*.

1943 Provided illustrations to Walt Whitman's *The Leaves of Grass* published by the Peter Pauper Press, Mount Vernon, New York, and to Mary O'Hara's *Thunderhead*, published by J. B. Lippincott. Publication of Laurence E. Schmeckebier's *John Steuart Curry's Pageant of America* by American Artists Group, New York.

1944 Provided illustrations to Stephen Crane's *The Red Badge of Courage*, published by The Heritage Press, New York.

1946 Traveled for three months to Cuba on assignment by the National City Bank, New York. Died of heart attack 29 August, in Madison, Wisconsin. One-man memorial exhibition held at the Milwaukee Art Institute, 5 September–15 October.

The Works of Grant Wood

Revolt Against the City
By Grant Wood

One year after joining the faculty at the University of Iowa, Grant Wood wrote a statement outlining his basic principles of art. The title of the essay, "Revolt Against the City," underlines its rhetorical promotion of regionalism, a movement to which artists all over the United States must, according to Wood, dedicate themselves in order to avoid a "colonial" dependency on European tradition. He felt that the rural Midwest—the farmer's life, dress, and setting—would provide the richest kind of material for a truly indigenous regionalist style. "Revolt Against the City" appeared as the first of four pamphlets edited and independently published in Iowa City in 1935 by Frank Luther Mott, a renowned journalism professor and historian of the press. Following the essay by Grant Wood, the short-lived "Whirling World Series" completed its brief run with three works by regional writers: an experimental "musical play" concerning a farm family entitled *Shroud My Body Down* by Paul Green, an interpretation in verse form of Chaucer's pilgrims by Edwin Ford Piper, entitled *Canterbury Pilgrims*, and a collection of poems devoted to rural life in Iowa by Hamlin Garland called *Iowa O Iowa*.

The present revolt against the domination exercised over art and letters and over much of our thinking and living by Eastern capitals of finance and politics brings up many considerations that ought to be widely discussed. It is no isolated phenomenon, and it is not to be understood without consideration of its historical, social, and artistic backgrounds. And though I am not setting out, in this essay, to trace and elaborate all of these backgrounds and implications, I wish to suggest a few of them in the following pages.

One reason for speaking out at this time lies in the fact that the movement I am discussing has come upon us rather gradually and without much blowing of trumpets, so that many observers are scarcely aware of its existence. It deserves, and I hope it may soon have, a much more thorough consideration than I give it here.

But if it is not vocal at least in the sense of issuing pronunciamentos, challenges, and new credos—the revolt is certainly very active. In literature, though by no means new, the exploitation of the "provinces" has increased remarkably; the South, the Middle West, the Southwest have at the moment hosts of interpreters whose Pulitzer-prize works and best sellers direct attention to their chosen regions. In drama, men like Paul Green, Lynn Riggs, and Jack Kirkland have been succeeding in something that a few years ago seemed impossible—actually interesting Broadway in something besides Broadway. In painting there has been a definite swing to a like regionalism; and this has been aided by such factors as the rejection of French domination, a growing consciousness of the art materials in the distinctively rural districts of America, and the system of PWA art work. These developments have correlations in the economic swing toward the country, in the back-to-the-land movement—that social phenomenon which Mr. Ralph Borsodi calls the "flight" from the city.

In short, America has turned introspective. Whether or not one adopts the philosophy of the "America Self-Contained" group, it is certain that the Depression Era has stimulated us to a re-evaluation of our resources in both art and economics, and that this turning of our eyes inward upon ourselves has awakened us to values which were little known before the grand crash of 1929 and which are chiefly non-urban.

This essay was first published in *Grant Wood: A Study in American Art*, by James M. Dennis

Mr. Carl Van Doren has pointed out the interesting fact that America rediscovers herself every thirty years or so. About once in each generation, directed by political or economic or artistic impulses, we have re-evaluated or reinterpreted ourselves. It happened in 1776, of course, and again a generation later with the Louisiana Purchase and subsequent explorations and the beginnings of a national literature. It came again with the expansion of the Jacksonian era in the eighteen-thirties, accompanied by a literary flowering not only in New England but in various frontier regions. It was marked in the period immediately after our Civil War, when Emerson observed that a new map of America had been unrolled before us. In the expansionist period at the turn of the century, shortly after the Spanish War when the United States found herself a full-fledged world power, we had a new discovery of resources and values. And now, with another thirty-year cycle, it comes again. It is always slightly different, always complex in its causes and phenomena; but happily it is always enlightening.

Moreover, these periods of national awakening to our own resources have always been in some degree reactions from foreign relationships. These reactions are obvious even to the casual reader of history and need not be listed here except as to their bearing on the present rediscovery. Economic and political causes have contributed in these days to turn us away from Europe—high tariff walls, repudiation of debts by European nations, the reaction against "entangling alliances" which followed upon President Wilson's effort to bring this country into the League of Nations, and the depression propaganda for "America Self-Contained."

But one does not need to be an isolationist to recognize the good which our artistic and literary secession from Europe has done us. For example, until fifteen years ago it was practically impossible for a painter to be recognized as an artist in America without having behind him the prestige of training either in Paris or Munich, while today the American artist looks upon a trip to Europe as any tourist looks upon it—not as a means of technical training or a method of winning an art reputation, but as a valid way to get perspective by foreign travel. This is a victory for American art of incalculable value. The long domination of our own art by Europe, and especially by the French, was a deliberately cultivated commercial activity—a business—and dealers connected with the larger New York galleries played into the hands of the French promoters because they themselves found such a connection profitable.

Music, too, labored under similar difficulties. Singers had to study in Germany or Italy or France; they had to sing in a foreign language, and they even had to adopt German or Italian or French names if they were to succeed in opera. In literature the language relationship made us subject especially to England. The whole of the nineteenth century was one long struggle to throw off that domination—a struggle more or less successful, but complicated in these later years by a continuation of the endless line of lionizing lecture tours of English authors and by the attempt to control our culture by the Rhodes scholarships which have been so widely granted.

This European influence has been felt most strongly in the Eastern States and particularly in the great Eastern seaport cities. René d'Harnoncourt, the Austrian artist who took charge of the Mexican art exhibit a few years ago and circulated it throughout the United States, and who probably has a clearer understanding of American art conditions than we do who are closer to them, believes that culturally our Eastern States are still colonies of Europe. The American artist of today, thinks d'Harnoncourt, must strive not so much against the French influence, which, after all, is merely incidental, but against the whole colonial influence which is so deep-seated in the New England States. The East is nearer to Europe in more than geographical position, and certain it is that the eyes of the seaport cities have long been focused upon the "mother" countries across the sea. But the colonial spirit is, of course, basically an imitative spirit, and we can have no hope of developing a culture of our own until that subserviency is put in its proper historical place.

Inevitable though it probably was, it seems nevertheless unfortunate that such art appreciation as developed in America in the nineteenth century had to be concentrated in the large cities. For the colonial spirit thereby was given full rein and control. The dominant factor in American social history during the latter part of that century is generally recognized as being the growth of large cities. D. R. Fox, writing an introduction to Arthur M. Schlesinger's "The Growth of the City," observes:

> The United States in the eighties and nineties was trembling between two worlds, one rural and agricultural, the other urban and industrial. In this span of years . . . traditional America gave way to a new America, one more akin to Europe than to its former self, yet retaining an authentic New World quality. . . . The present volume is devoted to describing and appraising the new social force which waxed and throve while driving the pioneer culture before it: the city.

This urban growth, whose tremendous power was so effective upon the whole of American society, served, so far as art was concerned, to tighten the grip of traditional imitativeness, for the cities were far less typically American than the frontier areas whose power they usurped. Not only were they the seats of the colonial spirit, but they were inimical to whatever was new, original, and alive in the truly American spirit.

Our Middle West, and indeed the "provinces" in general, have long had much the same attitude toward the East that the coastal cities had toward Europe. Henry James's journey to Paris as a sentimental pilgrim was matched by Hamlin Garland's equally passionate pilgrimage to Boston. It was a phase of the magnetic drawing-power of the Eastern cities that the whole country, almost up to the present time, looked wistfully eastward for culture; and these seaport centers drew unto them most of the writers, musicians, and artists who could not go on to Europe. And the flight of the "intelligentsia" to Paris was a striking feature of the years immediately after the World War.

The feeling that the East, and perhaps Europe, was the true goal of the seeker after culture was greatly augmented by the literary movement which Mr. Van Doren once dubbed "the revolt against the village." Such books as "Spoon River Anthology" and "Main Street" brought contempt upon the hinterland and strengthened the cityward tendency. H. L. Mencken's urban and European philosophy was exerted in the same direction.

But sweeping changes have come over American culture in the last few years. The Great Depression has taught us many things, and not the least of them is self-reliance. It has thrown down the Tower of Babel erected in the years of a false prosperity; it has sent men and women back to the land; it has caused us to rediscover some of the old frontier virtues. In cutting us off from traditional but more artificial values, it has thrown us back upon certain true and fundamental things which are distinctively ours to use and to exploit.

We still send scholars to Oxford, but it is significant that Paul Engle produced on his scholarship time one of the most American volumes of recent verse. Europe has lost much of its magic. Gertrude Stein comes to us from Paris and is only a seven days' wonder. Ezra Pound's new volume seems all compounded of echoes from a lost world. The expatriates do not fit in with the newer America, so greatly changed from the old.

The depression has also weakened the highly commercialized New York theatre; and this fact, together with the wholesome development of little theatres, may bring us at last an American drama. For years our stage has been controlled by grasping New York producers. The young playwright or actor could not succeed unless he went to New York. For commercial reasons, it was impossible to give the drama any regional feeling; it had little that was basic to go on and was consequently dominated by translations or reworkings of French plays and by productions of English drawing-room comedies, often played by imported actors. The advent of the movies changed this condition only by creating another highly urbanized center at Hollywood. But we have now a revolt against this whole system—a revolt in which we have enlisted the community theatres, local playwriting contests, some active regional playwrights, and certain important university theatres.

Music (and perhaps I am getting out of my proper territory here, for I know little of music) seems to be doing less outside of the cities than letters, the theatre, and art. One does note, however, local music festivals, as well as such promotion of community singing as that which Harry Barnhardt has led.

But painting has declared its independence from Europe, and is retreating from the cities to the more American village and country life. Paris is no longer the Mecca of the American artist. The American public, which used to be interested solely in foreign and imitative work, has readily acquired a strong interest in the distinctly indigenous art of its own land; and our buyers of paintings and patrons of art have naturally and honestly fallen in with the movement away from Paris and the American pseudo-Parisians. It all constitutes not so much a revolt against French technique as against the adoption of the French mental attitude and the use of French subject matter which he can best interpret because he knows it best, an American way of looking at things, and a utilization of the materials of our own American scene.

This is no mere chauvinism. If it is patriotic, it is so because a feeling for one's own milieu and for the validity of one's own life and its surroundings is patriotic. Certainly I prefer to think of it, not in terms of sentiment at all, but rather as a common-sense utilization for art of native materials—an honest reliance by the artist upon subject matter which he can best interpret because he knows it best.

Because of this new emphasis upon native materials, the artist no longer finds it necessary to migrate even to New York, or to seek any great metropolis. No longer is it necessary for him to suffer the confusing cosmopolitanism, the noise, the too intimate gregariousness of the large city. True, he may travel, he may observe, he may study in various environments, in order to develop his personality and achieve backgrounds and a perspective; but this need be little more than incidental to an educative process that centers in his own home region.

The great central areas of America are coming to be evaluated more and more justly as the years pass. They are not a Hinterland for New York; they are not barbaric. Thomas Benton returned to make his home in the Middle West just the other day, saying, according to the newspapers, that he was coming to live again in the only region of the country which is not "provincial." John Cowper Powys, bidding farewell to America recently in one of our great magazines, after a long sojourn in this country, said of the Middle West:

> This is the real America; this is—let us hope!—the America of the future; this is the region of what may, after all, prove to be, in Spenglerian phrase, the cradle of the next great human "culture."

When Christopher Morley was out in Iowa last Fall, he remarked on its freedom, permitting expansion "with space and relaxing conditions for work." Future artists, he wisely observed, "are more likely to come from the remoter areas, farther from the claims and distractions of an accelerating civilization."

So many of the leaders in the arts were born in small towns and on farms that in the comments and conversation of many who have "gone East" there is today a noticeable homesickness for the scenes of their childhood. On a recent visit to New York, after seven continuous years in the Middle West, I found this attitude very striking. Seven years ago my friends had sincerely pitied me for what they called my "exile" in Iowa. They then had a vision of my going back to an uninteresting region where I could have no contact with culture and no association with kindred spirits. But now, upon my return to the East, I found these same friends eager for news and information about the rich funds of creative material which this region holds.

I found, moreover, a determination on the part of some of the Eastern artists to visit the Middle West for the purpose of obtaining such material. I feel that, in general, such a procedure would be as false as the old one of going to Europe for subject matter, or the later fashion of going to New England fishing villages or to Mexican cities or to the mountains of our Southwest for materials. I feel that whatever virtue this new movement has lies in the necessity the painter (and the writer, too) is under, to use material which is really a part of himself. However, many New York artists and writers are more familiar, through strong childhood impressions, with village and country life than with their adopted urban environment; and for them a back-to-the-village movement is entirely feasible and defensible. But a cult or a fad for Midwestern materials is just what must be avoided. Regionalism has already suffered from a kind of cultism which is essentially false.

I think the alarming nature of the depression and the general economic unrest have had much to do in producing this wistful nostalgia for the Midwest to which I have referred. This region has always stood as the great conservative section of the country. Now, during boom times conservatism is a thing to be ridiculed, but under unsettled conditions it becomes a virtue. To the East, which is not in a position to produce its own food, the Middle West today looks a haven of security. This is, of course, the basis for the various projects for the return of urban populations to the land; but it is an economic condition not without implications for art. The talented youths who, in the expensive era of unlimited prosperity, were carried away on waves of enthusiasm for projects of various sorts, wanting nothing so much as to get away from the old things of home, now, when it all collapses, come back solidly to the good earth.

But those of us who have never deserted our own regions for long find them not so much havens of refuge, as continuing friendly, homely environments.

As for my own region—the great farming section of the Middle West—I find it, quite contrary to the prevailing Eastern impression, not a drab country inhabited by peasants, but a various, rich land abounding in painting material. It does not, however, furnish scenes of the picture-postcard type that one too often finds in New Mexico or further West, and sometimes in New England. Its material seems to me to be more sincere and honest, and to gain in depth by having to be hunted for. It is the result of analysis, and therefore is less obscured by "picturesque" surface quality. I find myself becoming rather bored by quaintness. I lose patience with the thinness of things viewed from outside, or from a height. Of course, my feeling for the genuineness of this Iowa scene is doubtless rooted in the fact that I was born here and have lived here most of my life. I shall not quarrel with the painter from New Mexico, from further West, or from quaint New England, if he differs with me; for if he does so honestly, he doubtless has the same basic feeling for his material that I have for mine—he believes in its genuineness. After all, all I contend for is the sincere use of native material by the artist who has command of it.

Central and dominant in our Midwestern scene is the farmer. The depression, with its farm strikes and the heroic attempts of Government to find solutions for agrarian difficulties, has emphasized for us all the fact that the farmer is basic in the economics of the country—and, further, that he is a human being. The farm strikes, strangely enough, caused little disturbance to the people of the Middle West who were not directly concerned in them; but they did cause both surprise and consternation in the East, far away as it is from the source of supplies. Indeed, the farm strikes did much to establish the Midwestern farmer in the Eastern estimation as a man, functioning as an individual capable of thinking and feeling, and not an oaf.

Midwestern farmers are not of peasant stock. There is much variety in their ancestry, of course; but the Iowa farmer as I know him is fully as American as Boston, and has the great advantage of being farther away from European influence. He knows little of life in crowded cities, and would find such intimacies uncomfortable; it is with difficulty that he reconciles himself even to village life. He is on a little unit of his own, where he develops an extraordinary independence. The economics, geography, and psychology of his situation have always accented his comparative isolation. The farmer's reactions must be toward weather, tools, beasts, and plants to a far greater extent than those of city dwellers, and toward other human beings far less: this makes him not an egoist by any means, but (something quite different) a less socialized being than the average American. The term "rugged individualism" has been seized upon as a political catchword, but it suits the farmer's character very well.

Of course, the automobile and the radio have worked some change in the situation; but they have not altered the farmer's essential character in this generation, whatever they may do in the next. More important so far as change is concerned have been recent economic conditions, including the foreclosing of mortgages; and these factors, threatening the farmer's traditional position as a self-supporting individual, threatening even a reduction to a kind of American peasantry, brought on the violent uprisings of the farm strikes and other protests.

The farmer is not articulate. Self-expression through literature and art belong not to the set of relationships with which he is familiar (those with weather, tools, and growing things), but to more socialized systems. He is almost wholly preoccupied with his struggle against the elements, with the fundamental things of life, so that he has no time for Wertherism or for the subtleties of interpretation. Moreover, the farmers that I know (chiefly of New England stock) seem to me to have something of that old Anglo-Saxon reserve which made our ancient forebears to look upon much talk about oneself as a childish weakness. Finally, ridicule by city folks with European ideas of the farmer as a peasant, or, as our American slang has it, a "hick," has caused a further withdrawal—a proud and disdainful answer to misunderstanding criticism.

But the very fact that the farmer is not himself vocal makes him the richest kind of material for the writer and the artist. He needs interpretation. Serious, sympathetic handling of farmer material offers a great field for the careful worker. The life of the farmer, engaged in a constant conflict with natural forces, is essentially dramatic. The drouth of last Summer provided innumerable episodes of the most gripping human interest. The nomadic movements of cattlemen in Wisconsin, in South Dakota, and in other states, the great dust storms, the floods following drouth, the milk strikes, the violent protests against foreclosures, the struggles against dry-year pests, the sacrifices forced upon once prosperous families—all these elements and many more are colorful, significant, and intensely dramatic.

It is a conflict quite as exciting as that of the fisherman with the sea. I have been interested to find in the little town of Waubeek, near my home, farmer-descendants of the folk of New England fishing villages. Waubeek has not changed or grown much since it was originally settled, because it was missed by the railroads and by the paved highways. The people of this community have kept as family heirlooms some of the old whaling harpoons, anchors, and so on which connect them with the struggle which their ancestors waged with the sea. But their own energies are transferred to another contest, and their crops come not out of the water but out of the land. I feel that the drama and color of the old fishing villages have become hackneyed and relatively unprofitable, while little has been done, in painting at least, with the fine materials that are inherent in farming in the great region of the Mid-American States.

My friend and fellow-townsman Jay Sigmund devotes his leisure hours to the writing of verse celebrating the kind of human beings I have been discussing. He is as much at home in Waubeek—perhaps more so—as in the office of his insurance company. I wish to quote a poem of his in this place.

Visitor

I knew he held the tang of stack and mow—
    One sensed that he was brother to the soil;
    His palms were stained with signs of stable toil
And calloused by the handles of the plow.

Yet I felt bound to him by many ties:
    I knew the countryside where he was born;
    I'd seen its hillsides green with rows of corn,
And now I saw its meadows in his eyes.

For he had kept deep-rooted in the clay,
    While I had chosen market-place and street;
    I knew the city's bricks would bruise his feet
And send him soon to go his plodding way.

But he had sought me out to grip my hand
    And sit for one short hour by my chair.
    Our talk was of the things that happen where
The souls of men have kinship with the land.

I asked him of the orchard and the grove,
    About the bayou with its reedy shore,
    About the grey one in the village store
Who used to doze beside a ruddy stove.

He told me how the creek had changed its bed,
    And how his acres spread across the hill;
    The hour wore on and he was talking still,
And I was hungry for the things he said.

Then I who long had pitied peasant folk
   And broken faith with field and pasture ground
   Felt dull and leaden-footed in my round,
And strangely like a cart-beast with a yoke!

There is, of course, no ownership in artistic subject matter except that which is validated by the artist's own complete apprehension and understanding of the materials. By virtue of such validation, however, the farm and village matter of a given region would seem peculiarly to belong to its own regional painters. This brings up the whole of the ancient moot question of regionalism in literature and art.

Occasionally I have been accused of being a flag-waver for my own part of the country. I do believe in the Middle West—in its people and in its art, and in the future of both—and this with no derogation to other sections. I believe in the Middle West in spite of abundant knowledge of its faults. Your true regionalist is not a mere eulogist; he may even be a severe critic. I believe in the regional movement in art and letters (comparatively new in the former though old enough in the latter); but I wish to place no narrow interpretation on such regionalism. There is, or at least there need be, no geography of the art mind or of artistic talent or appreciation. But painting and sculpture do not raise up a public as easily as literature, and not until the break-up caused by the Great Depression has there really been an opportunity to demonstrate the artistic potentialities of what some of our Eastern city friends call "the provinces."

Let me try to state the basic idea of the regional movement. Each section has a personality of its own, in physiography, industry, psychology. Thinking painters and writers who have passed their formative years in these regions will, by care-taking analysis, work out and interpret in their productions these varying personalities. When the different regions develop characteristics of their own, they will come into competition with each other; and out of this competition a rich American culture will grow. It was in some such manner that Gothic architecture grew out of competition between different French towns as to which could build the largest and finest cathedrals. And indeed the French Government has sponsored a somewhat similar kind of competition ever since Napoleon's time.

The germ of such a system for the United States is to be found in the art work recently conducted under the PWA. This was set up by geographical divisions, and it produced remarkable results in the brief space of time in which it was in operation. I should like to see such encouragement to art work continued and expanded. The Federal Government should establish regional schools for art instruction to specially gifted students in connection with universities or other centers of culture in various sections.

In suggesting that these schools should be allied with the universities, I do not mean to commit them to pedantic or even strictly academic requirements. But I do believe that the general liberal arts culture is highly desirable in a painter's training. The artist must know more today than he had to know in former years. My own art students, for example, get a general course in natural science—not with any idea of their specializing in biology or physics, but because they need to know what is going on in the modern world. The main thing is to teach students to think, and if they can to feel. Technical expression, though important, is secondary; it will follow in due time, according to the needs of each student. Because of this necessity of training in the liberal arts, the Government art schools should be placed at educational centers.

The annual exhibits of the work of schools of this character would arouse general interest and greatly enlarge our American art public. A local pride would be excited that might rival that which even hard-headed business men feel for home football teams and such enterprises. There is nothing ridiculous about such support; it would be only a by-product of a form of public art education which,when extended over a long period of time, would make us a great art-loving nation.

Mural painting is obviously well adapted to Government projects, and it is also highly suitable for regional expression. It enables students to work in groups, to develop original ideas under proper guidance, and to work with a very definite purpose. I am far from commending all the painting that has gone onto walls in the past year or two, for I realize there has not been much success in finding a style well suited to the steel-construction building; but these things will come, and there is sure to be a wonderful development in mural painting within the next few years. In it I hope that art students working with Government aid may play a large part. My students at the State University of Iowa hope to decorate the entire University Theatre, when the building is finished, in true fresco; and there is to be regional competition for the murals and sculpture in three new Iowa postoffices—at Dubuque, Ames, and Independence.

I am willing to go so far as to say that I believe the hope of a native American art lies in the development of regional art centers and the competition between them. It seems the one way to the building up of an honestly art-conscious America.

It should not be forgotten that regional literature also might well be encouraged by Government aid. Such "little" magazines as Iowa's *Midland* (now unfortunately suspended), Nebraska's *Prairie Schooner*, Oklahoma's *Space*, Montana's *Frontier* might well be subsidized so that they could pay their contributors. A board could be set up which could erect standards and allocate subsidies which would go far toward counteracting the highly commercialized tendencies of the great eastern magazines.

But whatever may be the future course of regional competitions, the fact of the revolt against the city is undeniable. Perhaps but few would concur with Thomas Jefferson's characterization of cities as "ulcers on the body politic"; but, for the moment at least, much of their lure is gone. Is this only a passing phase of abnormal times? Having at heart a deep desire for a widely diffused love for art among our whole people, I can only hope that the next few years may see a growth of non-urban and regional activity in the arts and letters.

97. *Old Sexton's Place*, ca. 1919, oil on composition board, 15 x 16 inches
Cedar Rapids Art Center, Mr. and Mrs. John B. Turner II Collection

98. *"Malnutrition": Portrait of Marvin Cone*, ca. 1919, oil on composition board, 13 x 11 inches
Private Collection

99. *The Runners: Luxembourg Gardens, Paris*, 1920, oil on composition board
15¾ x 12½ inches, Cedar Rapids Art Center, Bequest of Miss Nell Cherry

100. *Adoration of the Home*, 1921, oil on canvas, 28 x 81¼ inches
Cedar Rapids Art Center, Peter F. Bezanson Loan

101. *Fanciful Depiction of Roundhouse and Power Plant*, ca. 1920–1923, oil on canvas
35¼ x 72¾ inches, Cedar Rapids Art Center, St. Luke's Hospital Loan

102. *Autumn*, ca. 1922–1925, oil on composition board, 17 x 46 inches (lunette)
Cedar Rapids Art Center, Community School District Collection

103. *Winter*, ca. 1922–1925, oil on composition board, 20 x 39½ inches (lunette)
Cedar Rapids Art Center, Community School District Collection

104. *Spring*, ca. 1922–1925, oil on composition board, 10½ x 39½ inches (lunette)
Cedar Rapids Art Center, Community School District Collection

105. *Summer*, ca. 1922–1925, oil on composition board, 17 x 39½ inches (lunette)
Cedar Rapids Art Center, Community School District Collection

106. *Turner Mortuary, View from the Southwest*, 1924, pencil on paper, 18 x 29½ inches
Cedar Rapids Art Center, Mr. and Mrs. John B. Turner II Collection

107. *The Old J. G. Cherry Plant*, 1925, oil on composition board, 13 x 41 inches (arched top)
Cedar Rapids Art Center, Cherry-Burrell Foundation Collection

108. *Ten Tons of Accuracy*, 1925, oil on composition board, 22 x 36 inches
Cedar Rapids Art Center, Cherry-Burrell Foundation Collection

109. *Door at the Foot of the Stair*, 1927, oil on canvas, 24 x 18 inches
Cedar Rapids Art Center, Gift of the Artist, 1928

110. *Indian Creek, Autumn*, 1928, oil on composition board, 19 x 23⅛ inches
Private Collection, Cedar Rapids

111. *Vase of Zinnias*, ca. 1928–1929, oil on canvas, 22 x 22 inches
Cedar Rapids Art Center, Promised Gift, Collection of Gordon Fennell

112. *Black Barn*, 1929, oil on composition board, 9½ x 13 inches
Private Collection

113. *Woman with Plant*, 1929, oil on upson board, 20½ x 15 inches
Cedar Rapids Art Center, Purchase

114. *John B. Turner: Iowa Pioneer*, 1928–1930, oil on canvas, 30 x 25 inches
Cedar Rapids Art Center, Mr. and Mrs. John B. Turner II Collection

115. *Arnold Comes of Age*, 1930, oil on composition board, 26¾ x 23 inches
Nebraska Art Association, Lincoln, Nebraska

116. *Appraisal*, 1931, oil on composition board, 29½ x 35¼ inches
Carnegie-Stout Public Library

117. *Fall Plowing* (sketch), 1931, oil on masonite, 13¼ x 15¼ inches
Davenport Art Gallery

118. *Fall Plowing*, 1931, oil on canvas, 30 x 40¾ inches
John Deere and Company, Moline, Illinois

119. *The Birthplace of Herbert Hoover* (sketch), 1931, chalk and pencil on paper, 29⅜ x 39⅜ inches
Private Collection, Courtesy University of Iowa Museum of Art

120. *The First Three Degrees of Free Masonry*, 1931, oil on canvas triptych
25 (h) x 18 x 41 x 18 (w) inches, Masonic Temple, Cedar Rapids

121. *Self-Portrait* (sketch), 1932, oil on masonite, 13⅔ x 12⅜ inches
Davenport Art Gallery

122. *Spring Plowing*, 1932, oil on masonite panel, 18¼ x 22 inches
Private Collection

123. *Draft Horse*, 1933, pencil, charcoal, and chalk on brown wrapping paper, 16 x 21¾ inches (oval)
Cedar Rapids Art Center, Mrs. John B. Turner II

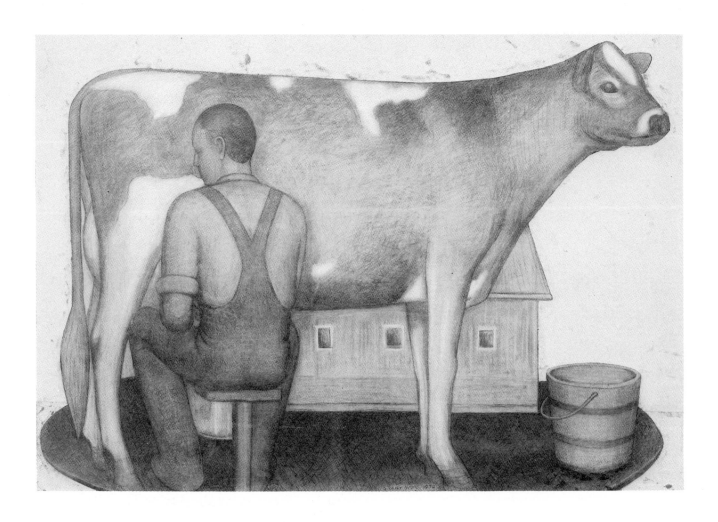

124. *Hired Hand Milking Cow*, 1931–1932, charcoal, pencil, and chalk on brown wrapping paper
38 x 54 inches, John Deere and Company, Moline, Illinois

126. *Farmer's Daughter*, 1931–1932, pencil, charcoal, and chalk on brown wrapping paper 54 x 21 inches, John Deere and Company, Moline, Illinois

125. *Fruits of Iowa: Farmer's Daughter*, 1932, oil on canvas, 47½ x 35⅛ inches
Coe College Collection, Cedar Rapids

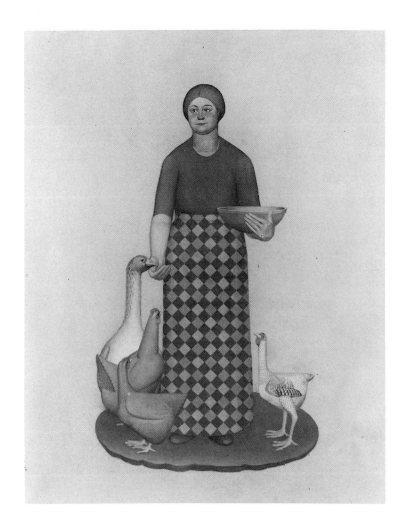

128. *Farmer's Wife with Chickens*, 1932, pencil, charcoal, and chalk on brown wrapping paper 54 x 37 inches, John Deere and Company, Moline, Illinois

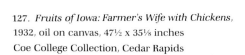

127. *Fruits of Iowa: Farmer's Wife with Chickens*, 1932, oil on canvas, 47½ x 35⅛ inches Coe College Collection, Cedar Rapids

129. *Fruits of Iowa: Farmer's Son*, 1932, oil on canvas, 47½ x 35⅛ inches
Coe College Collection, Cedar Rapids

130. *Trees and Hill*, 1933, oil on masonite, 30½ x 37 inches
Cedar Rapids Art Center, Community School District Collection

131. *Near Sundown*, 1933, oil on masonite, 15 x 26½ inches
Helen Foresman Spencer Museum of Art, University of Kansas, Promised Gift of George Cukor

132. *Dinner for Threshers* (left section), 1933, pencil and gouache on paper, 17¾ x 26¾ inches
Whitney Museum of American Art, New York

133. *Dinner for Threshers* (right section), 1933, pencil and gouache on paper, 17¾ x 26¾ inches
Whitney Museum of American Art, New York

134. *Adolescence* (sketch), ca. 1933–1934
Private Collection, Cedar Rapids

135. *Return from Bohemia*, 1935, pastel on paper, 23¾ x 20 inches
IBM Corporation, Armonk, New York

136. *Death on the Ridge Road*, 1935, oil on masonite, 32 x 39 inches
Williams College Museum of Art, Gift of Cole Porter, 1947

137. *Grandma Mending*, 1935, crayon, gouache, and colored pencil, 26¼ x 19½ inches
Hirschl and Adler Galleries, New York

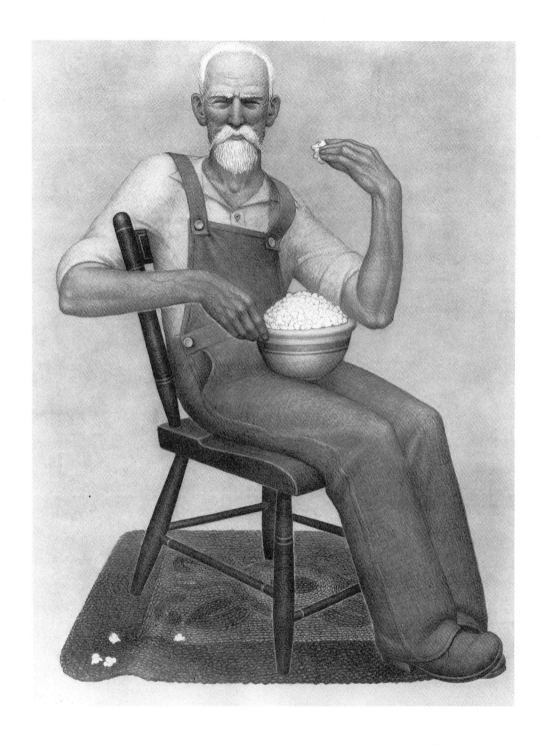

138. *Grandpa Eating Popcorn*, 1935, crayon, gouache, and colored pencil, 26¼ x 19½ inches
Hirschl and Adler Galleries, New York

139. *The Early Bird*, ca. 1936, crayon on paper, 5¾ x 6½ inches
Cedar Rapids Art Center, Community School District Collection

140. *Young Calf*, ca. 1936, crayon
on paper, 5¾ x 6½ inches
Cedar Rapids Art Center, Community
School District Collection

141. *The Escape*, ca. 1936, crayon
on paper, 5¾ x 6½ inches
Cedar Rapids Art Center, Community
School District Collection

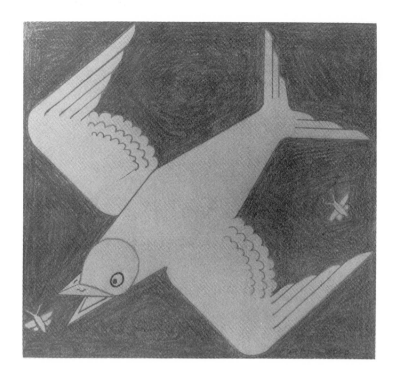

142. *Insect Suicide*, ca. 1936, crayon on paper, 5¾ x 6½ inches
Cedar Rapids Art Center, Community School District Collection

143. *Bold Bug*, ca. 1936, crayon on paper, 5¾ x 6½ inches
Cedar Rapids Art Center, Community School District Collection

144. *Spring Turning* (sketch), ca. 1936, charcoal and watercolor, 17½ x 39¾ inches

145. *Study for Breaking the Prairie*, ca. 1935–1939
Colored pencil, chalk, and pencil on brown wrapping paper, 22¾ x 80¼ inches
Whitney Museum of American Art, New York

146. *Good Influence*, 1937, pencil and watercolor on masonite, 20¼ x 16 inches
Pennsylvania Academy of the Fine Arts, Collections Fund Purchase

147. *Plowing on Sunday*, 1938, ink gouache and conte on brown wrapping paper, 18 x 17⅛ inches
Rhode Island School of Design, Gift of Mrs. Murry S. Danforth

148. *New Road*, 1939, oil on masonite, 15 x 16⅞ inches
Private Collection

149. *Haying*, 1939, oil on masonite, 14⅞ x 16¾ inches
Private Collection

150. *Spring in Town* (sketch), 1941, charcoal and pencil, 23¾ x 22 inches
Kennedy Galleries, Inc.

151. *Spring in the Country*, 1941, charcoal, pencil, and chalk, 23½ x 21½ inches
Private Collection, Cedar Rapids

152. *Iowa Cornfield*, 1941, oil on masonite, 13 x 14⅞ inches
Davenport Art Gallery

153. *Last Sketch*, 1941, oil on masonite, 13 x 15¾ inches
Davenport Art Gallery

154. *Cross-Eyed Man* (after Rembrandt), ca. 1920, monoprint, 4½ x 4¼ inches (W-1)*

GRANT WOOD — Program Design for "A Kiss for Cinderella" — C.R. Community Players — 1931

ISABEL O. STAMATS

155. *A Kiss for Cinderella*, 1931, woodcut, 8½ x 5⅞ inches (W-2)

156. *Tree-Planting Group*, 1937, lithograph, 8½ x 11 inches (W-3)

157. *Tree-Planting Group*, 1933, charcoal, pencil, and chalk, 34 x 39 inches (W-3)

158. *Seed Time and Harvest*, 1937, lithograph, 7½ x 12¼ inches (W-4)

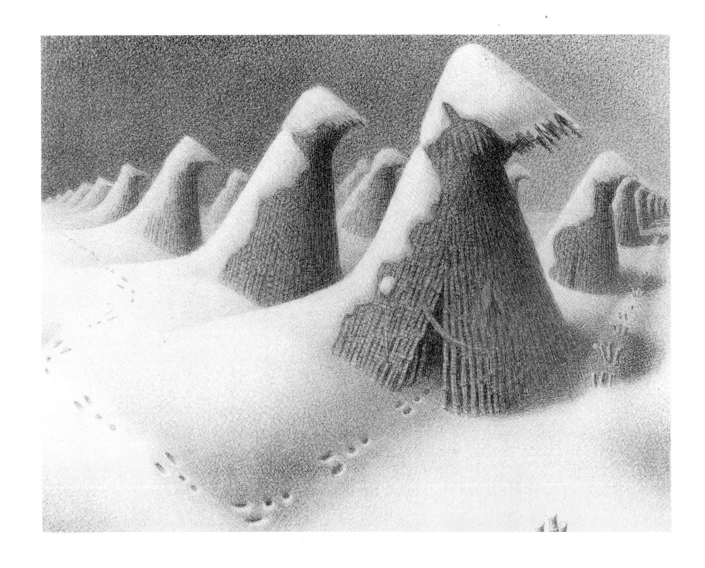

159. *January*, 1937, lithograph, 9 x 12 inches (W-5)

160. *January*, 1938, pencil, 18 x 24 inches (W-5)

161. *Sultry Night*, 1937, lithograph, 9¾ x 12¼ inches (W-6)

162. *Honorary Degree*, 1937, lithograph, 11¾ x 7 inches (W-7)

163. *Fruits*, 1938, lithograph,
9 x 12 inches (W-8)

164. *Tame Flowers*, 1938,
lithograph,
7 x 10 inches (W-9)

165. *Vegetables*, 1938, lithograph,
7 x 10 inches (W-10)

166. *Wild Flowers*, 1938,
lithograph, 7 x 10
inches (W-11)

167. *Fertility*, 1939, lithograph, 9 x 12 inches (W-12)

168. *Fertility*, 1939, charcoal, 17½ x 23½ inches (W-12)

169. *In the Spring*, 1939, lithograph, 9 x 12 inches (W-13)

170. *In the Spring*, 1939, pencil, 18 x 24 inches (W-13)

171. *July Fifteenth*, 1939, lithograph, 9 x 12 inches (W-14)

172. *Midnight Alarm*, 1939, lithograph, 12 x 7½ inches (W-15)

173. *Shriners' Quartet*, 1939, lithograph, 12 x 7¼ inches (W-16)

174. *Approaching Storm*, 1940, lithograph, 12 x 9 inches (W-17)

175. *March*, 1941, lithograph, 9 x 12 inches (W-18)

176. *February*, 1941, lithograph, 9 x 12 inches (W-19)

177. *December Afternoon*, 1941, lithograph, 9 x 12 inches (W-20)

178. *December Afternoon*, 1941, charcoal and pencil, 12 x 15¾ inches (W-20)

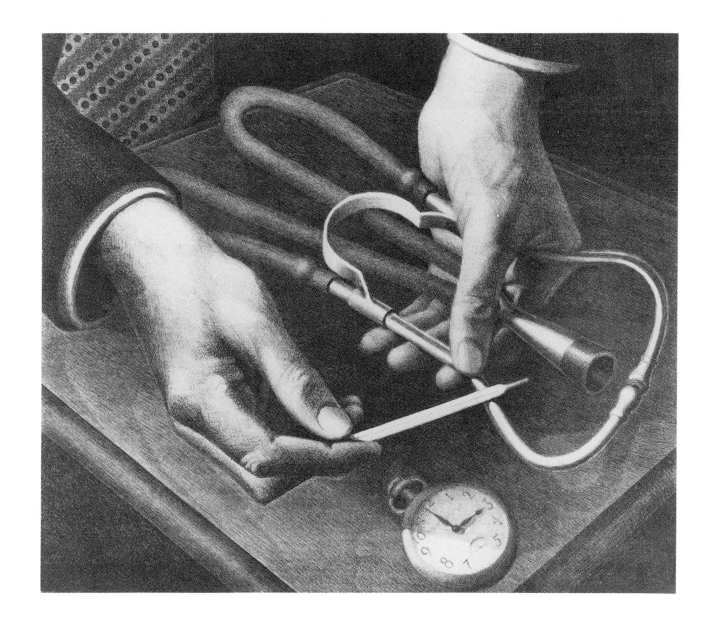

179. *Family Doctor*, 1941, lithograph, 10 x 12 inches (W-21)

W–1. *Cross-Eyed Man* (after Rembrandt), ca. 1920s (Figure 154)
Monoprint, 4½ x 4¼ inches
Collection: Mrs. Marvin Cone

W–2. *A Kiss for Cinderella*, 1931 (Figure 155)
Woodcut, 8½ x 5⅞ inches
Collection: Mrs. Herbert O. (Isabel) Stamats

W–3. *Tree-Planting Group*, 1937 (Figure 156)
Lithograph, 8½ x 11 inches
Edition of 250. Printed by George C. Miller on B.F.K. Rives. Published and distributed by Associated American Artists, New York.
Collections: CRAC, Dav, DMAC, FAMSF, Fogg, FWMA, MFAB, N–A, MBMA, Oberlin, PMA Smith, UI
Note: This print is similar in subject to a preliminary drawing in the collection of the Cedar Rapids Art Center (Figure 157). It is also related to a painting in oil on masonite panel (25 x 30 inches) in the collection of King Vidor, Beverly Hills, California.

W–4. *Seed Time and Harvest*, 1937 (Figure 158)
Lithograph, 7½ x 12¼ inches
Edition of 250. Printed by George C. Miller on B.F.K. Rives. Published and distributed by Associated American Artists, New York.
Collections: Amherst, Cornell, CRAC, Dav, DMAC, FAMSF, Kal, N–A, NYPL, Oberlin, Smith, UI, WAM, Wichita
Note: The location of preliminary sketches and drawings is unknown.

W–5. *January*, 1937 (Figure 159)
Alternate Titles: *January Snow*, *January Thaw*
Lithograph, 9 x 12 inches
Edition of 250. Printed by George C. Miller on B.F.K. Rives. Published and distributed by Associated American Artists, New York.
Collections: BMAG, CI, CMA, CRAC, Dart, Dav, DMAC, FAMSF, Fogg, MFAB, NBMA, Princeton
Note: This print is similar in subject to a drawing, Figure 160. It is also related to a painting in oil on masonite panel (18 x 24 inches) dated 1940 in the collection of King Vidor, Beverly Hills, California.

W–6. *Sultry Night*, 1937 (Figure 161)
Alternate Title: *Saturday Night Bath*
Lithograph, 9¾ x 12¼ inches
Edition of about 100. Printed by George C. Miller on B.F.K. Rives. Published and distributed by Associated American Artists, New York.
Collections: Amherst, CRAC, Dav, DMAC, MMA, NBMA
Note: This print is similar in subject to a drawing in charcoal (19 x 23 inches) dated 1937 in a private collection (Dennis, p. 185). An edition of 250 was planned, but the United States Post Office banned transit of the print through the mails.

W–7. *Honorary Degree*, 1937 (Figure 162)
Lithograph, 11¾ x 7 inches
Edition of 250. Printed by George C. Miller on B.F.K. Rives. Published and distributed by Associated American Artists, New York.
Collections: BMAG, CI, DAM, Dart, DMAC, FAMSF, Fogg, LC, MFAB, MOMA, NBMA, NYPL, PMA, UI, UM
Note: This print is similar in subject to a drawing in lithographic crayon and wash dated 1939 (?), included in sale 3585, Sotheby-Parke-Bernet, Inc., New York, December 13–14, 1973, No. 58. The figures represented are Dean Emeritus Carl W. Seashore of the Graduate College

(right), Grant Wood (center), and Professor Norman Foerster of the School of Letters (left), all of the University of Iowa.

W–8. *Fruits*, 1938 (Figure 163)
Lithograph, 9 x 12 inches
Edition of 250. Printed by George S. Miller on B.F.K. Rives. Published and distributed by Associated American Artists, New York.
Collections: CRAC, Dart, Dav, DMAC, HMA
Note: Although advertised as hand colored by the artist, the color tinting was done by Grant Wood's sister and her husband, Nan and Edward Graham, on Wood's instructions. The Davenport Art Gallery has a complete set that was hand tinted by Grant Wood. The location of preliminary sketches and drawings is unknown.

W–9. *Tame Flowers*, 1938 (Figure 164)
Lithograph, 7 x 10 inches
Edition of 250. Printed by George C. Miller on B. F. K. Rives. Published and distributed by Associated American Artists, New York.
Collections: CRAC, Dav, DMAC
Note: Although advertised as hand colored by the artist, the color tinting was done by Grant Wood's sister and her husband, Nan and Edward Graham, on Wood's instructions. The Davenport Art Gallery has a complete set that was hand tinted by Grant Wood. The location of preliminary sketches and drawings is unknown.

W–10. *Vegetables*, 1938 (Figure 165)
Lithograph, 7 x 10 inches
Edition of 250. Printed by George C. Miller on B.F.K. Rives. Published and distributed by Associated American Artists, New York.
Collections: CRAC, Dav, DMAC, HMA, UM
Note: Although advertised as hand colored by the artist, the color tinting was done by Grant Wood's sister and her husband, Nan and Edward Graham, on Wood's instructions. The Davenport Art Gallery has a complete set that was hand tinted by Grant Wood. The location of preliminary sketches and drawings is unknown.

W–11. *Wild Flowers*, 1938 (Figure 166)
Lithograph, 7 x 10 inches
Edition of 250. Printed by George C. Miller on B.F.K. Rives. Published and distributed by Associated American Artists, New York.
Collections: Amherst, CRAC, Dav, DMAC
Note: Although advertised as hand colored by the artist, the color tinting was done by Grant Wood's sister and her husband, Nan and Edward Graham, on Wood's instructions. The Davenport Art Gallery has a complete set that was hand tinted by Grant Wood. The location of preliminary sketches and drawings is unknown.

W–12. *Fertility*, 1939 (Figure 167)
Lithograph, 9 x 12 inches
Edition of 250. Printed by George C. Miller on B.F.K.Rives. Published and distributed by Associated American Artists, New York.
Collections: Amherst, BMAG, CI, CRAC, Dav, DMAC, FAMSF, Fogg, Kal, MFAB, MMA, NBMA, NCFA, Okl, UI, UM
Note: This print is similar in subject to a preliminary drawing, Figure 168, in the collection of Kennedy Galleries, Inc.

W–13. *In the Spring*, 1939 (Figure 169)
Lithograph, 9 x 12 inches

Edition of 250. Printed by George C. Miller on B.F.K. Rives. Published and distributed by Associated American Artists, New York.
Collections: AIC, Amherst, Bklyn, BMAG, CI, CRAC, Dart, Dav, DMAC, FAMSF, MFAB, MMA, NBMA, NCFA, Wichita
Note: This print is similar in subject to a preliminary drawing, Figure 170, in the collection of the Butler Institute of American Art.

W–14. *July Fifteenth*, 1939 (Figure 171)
Alternate Title: *Summer Landscape*
Lithograph, 9 x 12 inches
Edition of 250. Printed by George C. Miller on B.F.K. Rives. Published and distributed by Associated American Artists, New York.
Collections: CRAC, Dav, DMAC, FAMSF, Fogg, Kal, MFAB
Note: The location of preliminary drawings or sketches is unknown.

W–15. *Midnight Alarm*, 1939 (Figure 172)
Lithograph, 12 x 7½ inches
Edition of 250. Printed by George C. Miller on B.F.K. Rives. Published and distributed by Associated American Artists, New York.
Collections: Amherst, BMAG, CI, CRAC, Dart, Dav, DMAC, FAMSF, Flint, Fogg, MFAB, MMA, UM, Yale
Note: The location of preliminary drawings or sketches is unknown.

W–16. *Shriners' Quartet*, 1939 (Figure 173)
Lithograph, 12 x 7¼ inches
Edition of 250. Printed by George C. Miller on B.F.K. Rives. Published and distributed by Associated American Artists, New York.
Collections: BMAG, CI, CRAC, Dart, Dav, DMAC, FAMSF, LC, MMA, MOMA, NBMA, Princeton, UI, Wichita
Note: The location of preliminary drawings or sketches is unknown.

W–17. *Approaching Storm*, 1940 (Figure 174)
Lithograph, 12 x 9 inches
Edition of 250. Printed by George C. Miller on B.F.K. Rives. Published and distributed by Associated American Artists, New York.
Collections: BMAG, CI, CRAC, Dav, DMAC, FAMSF, Fogg, LC, MFAB, NMBA, Princeton, UM
Note: This print is similar in subject to a drawing in pencil and charcoal dated 1940 in a private collection (dimensions unavailable).

W–18. *March*, 1941 (Figure 175)
Lithograph, 9 x 12 inches
Edition of 250. Printed by George C. Miller on B.F.K. Rives. Published and distributed by Associated American Artists, New York.
Collections: Bklyn, BMAG, CI, CRAC, Dav, DMAC, FAMSF, Fogg, Kal, LC, MFAB, NBMA, UI, UM
Note: This print is similar in subject to a drawing in charcoal (18 x 23 inches) dated 1940 in the collection of the Davenport Art Gallery.

W–19. *February*, 1941 (Figure 176)
Lithograph, 9 x 12 inches
Edition of 250. Printed by George C. Miller on B.F.K. Rives. Published and distributed by Associated American Artists, New York.
Collections: BMAG, CI, CRAC, Dav, DMAC, FAMSF, HMA, MFAB, MMA, NBMA, UI, UM, UN, Wichita
Note: The location of preliminary drawings or sketches is unknown. However, in the May 1942 *Demcourier*, a listing of "The Important Works by Grant Wood" includes a crayon drawing dated 1941 in the collection of Mrs. Elon Huntington Hooker, New York.

W–20. *December Afternoon*, 1941 (Figure 177)
Lithograph, 9 x 12 inches
Edition of 250. Printed by George C. Miller on B.F.K. Rives. Published and distributed by Associated American Artists, New York.
Collections: Amherst, BMAG, CRAC, Dart, Dav, DMAC, FAMSF, Fogg, LC, MFAB, UI, UM
Note: This print is similar in subject to a drawing, Figure 188, in the collection of the University of Iowa Museum of Art.

W–21. *Family Doctor*, 1941 (Figure 179)
Lithograph, 10 x 12 inches
Edition of 300. Printed by George C. Miller on B.F.K. Rives. Published and distributed by Abbott Laboratories, Chicago, Illinois.
Collections: AIC, CRAC, Dart, Dav, DMAC, MFAB
Note: The location of preliminary drawings or sketches is unknown. The hands represented were those of Wood's physician, Dr. A. W. Bennett, Iowa City.

Chronology: Grant Wood

1891   Born 13 February on a farm near Anamosa, Iowa, the second of four children of Quaker parents, Francis M. (date unknown–1901) and Hattie D. Weaver Wood (dates unknown).

1901   After death of father (March), Mrs. Wood moved from Anamosa farm, in September, with the four children to Cedar Rapids, Iowa, about twenty-five miles away.

1904–1908   Began earliest work in watercolor foliage and landscape elements. Provided illustration of *Graduating Seniors, 1908* for Washington High School yearbook.

1910   Graduated from Washington High School, Cedar Rapids, in June. Immediately traveled to Minneapolis and entered the summer term of the Minneapolis School of Design, Handicraft, and Normal Art to study design with Ernest A. Batchelder (dates unknown). Author of the book *The Principles of Design* (Chicago, 1904), Batchelder was a frequent contributor to *The Craftsman* and a leading advocate of the English Arts and Crafts movement.

1911   Enrolled for a second summer term in Minneapolis with Ernest A. Batchelder.

1911–1912   Taught classes at Rosedale Country School near Cedar Rapids. Attended night class in life drawing by Charles A. Cumming (dates unknown) at the University of Iowa, Iowa City.

1913   Moved to Chicago in spring and worked as a designer at Kale Silversmith Shop. Began night classes in October at the School of the Art Institute of Chicago. Remained through 19 January 1915. Lived at 3550 Ellis Ave.

1914–1915   Established partnership in June with fellow Kale craftsman, Christopher Haga. Opened the Wolund Shop in Park Ridge, specialized in jewelry design. Business failed late in 1915.

1916   Enrolled for two weeks in the day school of the Art Institute of Chicago. Returned to Cedar Rapids in late January, painted signs and did interior decorating to subsist. Occupied temporary quarters with mother and sister on a bluff overlooking Indian Creek in Kenwood Heights.

1917   Completed new house at 3118 Grove Court, S.E., on a lot given him by Paul Hanson in return for his labor.

1917–1918   Entered army, initially stationed at Camp Dodge, Iowa, then transferred to Washington, D.C., where he designed camouflage scenes for artillery.

1919   Returned to Cedar Rapids and in September began teaching art at Jackson High School, where Miss Frances Prescott was principal. Together with Marvin D. Cone (1891–1965), Wood exhibited twenty-three small panel paintings of barns, out-buildings, and tree landscapes at Killians Department Store, 9–22 October.

1920   Traveled to Paris in summer with Marvin D. Cone, lived in a pension on square de l'Abeille, boulevard Port-Royal. Resumed teaching responsibilities at Jackson High School. Exhibited with Marvin D. Cone thirty-one Paintings of Paris at the Library Art Gallery, Cedar Rapids, 10–20 November.

1921   Completed *First Three Degrees of Free Masonry* for the Masonic Library, Anamosa; subsequently transferred in 1940 to the Masonic Library, Cedar Rapids.

1922   Due to position change of Miss Frances Prescott, Wood also transfers to McKinley High School in September. Completed outdoor mural *The Adoration of the Home* (28 × 81¼ inches) for Henry S. Ely and Company, Realtors.

1923   Traveled to Paris in autumn and attended Académie Julien on rue du Dragon. Worked in Sorrento, Italy, during winter 1923–1924, holding exhibit-sale of his paintings at the Hotel Coccumello.

1924   Returned to Paris in spring after winter in Sorrento, Italy. Remained through summer and painted Paris and French provinces. Returned to Cedar Rapids in autumn to temporarily resume teaching at McKinley High School. Moved into the carriage house of the George B. Douglas mansion; currently being converted into the Mortuary of John B. Turner and Son. Wood provided a series of thirteen pencil and ink drawings of the new mortuary (at Second Avenue and Eighth), of which five were published in an information brochure dated 12 December. Adopted address No. 5 Turner Alley.

1925   Retired from public school teaching, May. Completed series of commissions for J. G. Cherry Plant, Cedar Rapids, a manufacturer of dairy equipment that dealt with the theme of quality through craftsmanship. Seven oil on upson board paintings were completed (Cedar Rapids Art Center). Continued doing interior decorating for several Cedar Rapids families.

1926   Traveled to Europe in June and July, painting in Paris and southern France. Exhibited forty-seven paintings of medieval doorways and gates at Galerie Carmine, rue de Seine, Paris, July. Subsequently exhibited many of these works at the Public Library Gallery, Cedar Rapids, December.

1927   Received commission in January to design stained glass window for the Veterans Memorial Building, Cedar Rapids. Worked with artist Arnold Pyle (1908–1973) mounting a full-scale drawing in Quaker Oats Plant of 288 × 240 inches on fifty-eight sections. Traveled in summer with David Turner to Estes Park, Colorado. Developed and completed a series of oil on canvas (72 × 288 inches) murals for the Hotel Chieftain, Council Bluffs, Iowa. Intended for the

Corn Room, the murals, of which only fragments remain in a private collection, depict the Mormon settlement of Kanesville, later Council Bluffs, in 1849.

1928   Veterans Memorial Building commission approved January. Firm of Emil Frei, St. Louis, retained to assemble the window. Traveled to Munich in September to supervise the manufacture in glass of his design. Especially fascinated by Flemish and German old masters and their choice of subject matter. Final visit abroad.

1928–1930   Completed *John B. Turner: Iowa Pioneer* (Figure 114).

1929   Veterans Memorial Building Window installed, March. Completed portrait of his mother at age 71, *Woman with Plant* (Figure 113).

1930   Completed painting *Stone City, Iowa* (Figure 10), *American Gothic* (Figure 14), and *Overmantel Decoration* (Figure 13). Representing his sister Nan and dentist Dr. B. H. McKeeby, *American Gothic* awarded Norman Walt Harris Bronze Medal and Purchase Prize at the 43rd Annual Exhibition of American Painting and Sculpture at the Art Institute, Chicago, 30 October–14 November. Painting was an instant success and established Wood's reputation as an American painter.

1931   Completed *The Birthplace of Herbert Hoover* (Figure 9), *Midnight Ride of Paul Revere* (30 × 40 inches, Metropolitan Museum of Art), *Fall Plowing* (Figure 118), *Victorian Survival* (32½ × 26¼ inches, Carnegie-Stout Public Library), *Young Corn* (Figure 17), among others.

1932   Completed *Daughters of Revolution* (20 × 40 inches, Cincinnati Art Museum) and *Arbor Day* (Figure 11), among others. Helped establish the Stone City Colony and Art School, 26 June–6 August. Accredited through Coe College (Cedar Rapids), Stone City was sponsored by the Iowa Artist's Club in cooperation with the Little Gallery (Cedar Rapids Art Association) project of the American Federation of Arts. Located in the Valley of the Wapsipinicon River, Stone City is twenty-six miles from Cedar Rapids and three miles from Anamosa. Faculty included Marvin D. Cone and Edward B. Rowan (1898–1946). Commissioned in 1931, the *Fruits of Iowa* murals (seven—Coe College Library, Figures 127, 129) were installed in 1932 in the Montrose Hotel Dining Room.

1933   Completed several distinguished landscapes including *Near Sundown* (Figure 131) and *Trees and Hill* (30½ × 37 inches, Cedar Rapids Art Center). Continued the Stone City Colony and Art School, 27 June–22 August. Met John S. Curry for the first time, when he visited Stone City, July. Completed a series of five charcoal drawings (32 × 42 inches average) for *The Art of Writing*, Chicago, A. N. Palmer Company, to be exhibited at the World's Fair.

1934   Appointed director of Public Works of Art Project in Iowa City and supervised completion by fourteen artists at Iowa City of murals for the Iowa State University Library, Ames. Completed *Dinner for Threshers* (Figure 15), provided book jacket illustrations for Vardis Fisher's *In Tragic Life* and *Passion Spins the Plot*. Became associate professor of Fine Arts at the University of Iowa. Lectured extensively.

1935   Provided book jacket illustration for Thomas Duncan's *O Chautauqua* (180 × 14¼ inches, private collection). Married Sara Sherman Maxon 2 March and purchased a home in Iowa City. Completed *Death on Ridge Road* (Figure 136). Elected to the National Society of Mural Painters. One-man exhibits at The Lakeside Press Galleries, Chicago, February–March, and Ferargil Galleries, New York, 15 April–15 May. Death of his mother, Hattie Weaver Wood. "Revolt Against the City" published in Iowa City by Frank Luther Mott.

1936   Completed *Spring Turning* (18⅛ × 40 inches, private collection, see sketch, Figure 144). Provided twenty crayon and gouache illustrations for Madeliene Darrough Horn's *Farm on the Hill* (New York: Charles Scribner's Sons). Awarded Honorary Doctor of Letters from University of Wisconsin, Madison. One-man exhibit at Walker Gallery, New York, April–May.

1937   Completed series of drawings in charcoal, pencil, and chalk (20½ × 16 inches) begun in 1935 for a publication of Sinclair Lewis's *Main Street*, Limited Editions Club. Installed 16 June a final three-panel oil on canvas mural depicting pioneer farmers clearing virgin land, in the lower lobby of the Iowa State University Library. As in earlier murals, the actual painting was done by a group of students after designs and sketches by Wood. Preliminary drawing of charcoal, pencil on paper (23 [h] × 16½ × 45 × 16½ inches) entitled *When Tillage Begins* (see study, Figure 145). Began work in lithography, completed 5 prints.

1938   Provided book jacket illustration (pencil, ink, gouache, 23 × 21 inches) for Sterling North's *Plowing on Sunday* (Figure 147). Summered at Clear Lake. Received honorary degree from Lawrence College, Appleton, Wisconsin. Separated from Sara Maxon Wood.

1939   Divorced Sara Maxon Wood. Completed *Parson Weem's Fable* (38⅜ × 50⅛ inches, Amon Carter Museum of Art).

1940   Provided book jacket illustration for Kenneth Roberts's *Oliver Wiswell*. Completed *Sentimental Ballad* (24 × 51 inches, New Britain Museum of American Art), based on the film version of Eugene O'Neill's *The Long Voyage Home*. Further details can be found in *American Artist* 4 (September 1940): 4–14. Had one year sabbatical from his position at the University of Iowa. Lectured extensively, including presentations at UCLA and the University of California on regional painting.

1941   Appointed full professor of fine arts at the University of Iowa, Iowa City. Completed paintings *Spring in Town* (Figure 12) and *Spring in the Country* (Cornelius Vanderbilt Whitney Collection) at his summer Clear Lake studio. Awarded honorary degree from Northwestern University, Evanston, Illinois, and awarded honorary degree from Wesleyan University, Middletown, Connecticut.

1942   Died 12 February of cancer at University of Iowa Hospital. Interred at Riverside Cemetery, Anamosa, Iowa. Memorial exhibition held at the Art Institute of Chicago, 29 October–December.

Afterword: On Regionalism, 1951
By Thomas Hart Benton

Here as I approach the end of my public adventures, I must go back a little and pick up an association which was for a time very much involved in them. I have neglected to mention the two artists whose names during the days of success were always connected with mine. John Steuart Curry and Grant Wood rose along with me to public attention in the thirties. They were very much a part of what I stood for and made it possible for me in my lectures and interviews to promote the idea that an indigenous art with its own aesthetics was a growing reality in America. Without them, I would have had only personal grounds to stand on for my pronouncements.

We were, the three of us, pretty well along before we ever became acquainted or were linked under the now famous name of Regionalism. We were different in our temperaments and many of our ideas, but we were alike in that we were all in revolt against the unhappy effects which the Armory show of 1913 had had on American painting. We objected to the new Parisian aesthetics which was more and more turning art away from the living world of active men and women into an academic world of empty pattern. We wanted an American art which was not empty, and we believed that only by turning the formative processes of art back again to meaningful subject matter, in our cases specifically American subject matter, could we expect to get one.

A book like this, devoted so much to personal happenings, is hardly one in which to deal extensively with the ideas underlying our Regionalism so I shall reserve a detailed study of that for another writing. The term was, so to speak, wished upon us. Borrowed from a group of southern writers who were interested in their regional cultures, it was applied to us somewhat loosely, but with a fair degree of appropriateness. However, our interests were wider than the term suggests. They had their roots in that general and countrywide revival of Americanism which followed the defeat of Woodrow Wilson's universal idealism at the end of World War One and which developed through the subsequent periods of boom and depression until the new internationalisms of the Second World War pushed it aside. This Americanist period had many facets, some dark, repressive and suggestive of an ugly neo-fascism, but on the whole it was a time of general improvement in democratic idealism. After the break of 1929 a new and effective liberalism grew over the country and the battles between that liberalism and the entrenched moneyed groups, which had inherited our post Civil War sociology and were in defense of it, brought out a new and vigorous discussion of the intended nature of our society. This discussion and the political battles over its findings, plus a new flood of historical writing concentrated the thirties on our American image. It was this countrywide concentration more probably than any of our artistic efforts which raised Wood, Curry, and me to prominence in the national scene. We symbolized aesthetically what the majority of Americans had in mind—America itself. Our success was a popular success. Even where some American citizens did not agree with the nature of our images, instanced in the objections to my state-sponsored murals in Indiana and Missouri, they understood them. What ideological battles we had were in American terms and were generally comprehensible to Americans as a whole. This was exactly what we wanted. The fact that our art was arguable in the language of the street, whether or not it was liked, was

This essay was first published in *An Artisan America*, by Thomas Hart Benton.

proof to us that we had succeeded in separating it from the hothouse atmospheres of an imported and, for our country, functionless aesthetics. With that proof we felt that we were on the way to releasing American art from its subservience to borrowed forms. In the heyday of our success, we really believed we had at last succeeded in making a dent in American aesthetic colonialism.

However, as later occurrences have shown, we were well off the beam on that score. As soon as the Second World War began substituting in the public mind a world concern for the specifically American concerns which had prevailed during our rise, Wood, Curry, and I found the bottom knocked out from under us. In a day when the problems of America were mainly exterior, our interior images lost public significance. Losing that, they lost the only thing which could sustain them because the critical world of art had, by and large, as little use for our group front as it had for me as an individual. The coteries of highbrows, of critics, college art professors, and museum boys, the tastes of which had been thoroughly conditioned by the new aesthetics of twentieth-century Paris, had sustained themselves in various subsidized ivory towers and kept their grip on the journals of aesthetic opinion all during the Americanist period. These coteries, highly verbal but not always notably intelligent or able to see through momentarily fashionable thought patterns, could never accommodate our popularist leanings. They had, as a matter of fact, a vested interest in aesthetic obscurity, in highfalutin symbolisms and devious and indistinct meanings. The entertainment of these obscurities, giving an appearance of superior discernment and extraordinary understanding, enabled them to milk the wealthy ladies who went in for art and the college and museum trustees of the country for the means of support. Immediately after it was recognized that Wood, Curry, and I were bringing American art out into a field where its meanings had to be socially intelligible to justify themselves and where aesthetic accomplishment would depend on an effective representation of cultural ideas, which were themselves generally comprehensible, the ivory tower boys and girls saw the danger to their presumptions and their protected positions. They rose with their supporting groups of artists and highbrowish disciples to destroy our menace.

As I have related, I profited greatly by their fulminations and so, for a while, did Wood and Curry. However, in the end they succeeded in destroying our Regionalism and returning American art to that desired position of obscurity, and popular incomprehensibility which enabled them to remain its chief prophets. The Museum of Modern Art, the Rockefeller-supported institution in New York, and other similar culturally rootless artistic centers, run often by the most neurotic of people, came rapidly, as we moved through the war years, to positions of predominant influence over the artistic life of our country. As the attitudes of these cultist groups were grounded on aesthetic events which had occurred or were occurring in cultures overseas their ultimate effect was to return American art to the imitative status from which Wood, Curry, and I had tried to extricate it. The younger artists of America were left, in this situation, only with an extenuating function. The sense of this humiliating state of affairs led many of them, and notably some of the most talented of my old students, to a denial of all formal values and they began pouring paint out of cans and buckets just to see what would happen or tieing pieces of wire to sticks and smacking them around in the air in the name of a new mobility. This American contribution to "modern" aesthetics, though it suggests the butler trying to outdo his master's manners, received wide applause in our cultist circles and it went out from there to the young ladies' colleges and to the small-town art schools and into the minds of all those thousands of amateurs over the land who took themselves to be artists. These latter saw immediately the wonderful opportunities for their own ego advancement which this "free expression" afforded and embraced it enthusiastically.

Now all this anarchic idiocy of the current American art scene cannot be blamed solely on the importation of foreign ideas about art or on the existence in our midst of institutions which represent them. It is rather that our artists have not known how to deal with these. In other fields than art, foreign ideas have many times vastly benefited our culture. In fact few American ideas are wholly indigenous, nor in fact are those of any other country, certainly not in our modern world. But most of the imported ideas which have proved of use to us were able to become so by intellectual assimilation. They were thoughts which could be thought of. The difficulty in the case of aesthetic ideas is that intellectual assimilation is not enough—for effective production. Effective aesthetic production depends on something beyond thought. The intellectual aspects of art are not art nor does a comprehension of them enable art to be made. It is in fact the over-intellectualization of modern art and its separation from ordinary life intuitions which have permitted it, in this day of almost wholly collective action, to remain psychologically tied to the "public be damned" individualism of the last century and thus in spite of its novelties to represent a cultural lag.

Art has been treated by most American practitioners as if it were a form of science where like processes give like results all over the world. By learning to carry on the processes by which imported goods were made, the American artist assumed that he would be able to end with their expressive values. This is not perhaps wholly his fault because a large proportion of the contemporary imports he studied were themselves laboratory products, studio experiments in process, with pseudo-scientific motivations which suggested that art was, like science, primarily a process evolution. This put inventive method rather than a search for the human meaning of one's life at the center of artistic endeavor and made it appear that aesthetic creation was a matter for intellectual rather than intuitive insight. Actually this was only illusory and art's modern flight from representation to technical invention has only left it empty and stranded in the back waters of life. Without those old cultural ties which used to make the art of each country so expressive of national and regional character, it has lost not only its social purpose but its very techniques for expression.

It was against the general cultural inconsequence of modern art and the attempt to create by intellectual assimilation that Wood, Curry, and I revolted in the early twenties and turned ourselves to a reconsideration of artistic aims. We did not do this by agreement. We came to our conclusions separately but we ended with similar convictions that we must find our aesthetic values, not in thinking, but in penetrating to the meaning and forms of life as lived. For us this meant, as I have indicated, American life and American life as known and felt by ordinary Americans. We believed that only by our own participation in the reality of American life, and that very definitely included the folk patterns which sparked it and largely directed its assumptions, could we come to forms in which Americans would find an opportunity for genuine spectator participation. This latter, which we were, by the example of history, led to believe was a corollary, and in fact, a proof of real artistic vitality in a civilization, gave us that public-minded orientation which so offended those who lived above, and believed that art should live above, "vulgar" contacts. The philosophy of our popularism was rarely considered by our critics. It was much easier, especially after international problems took popular press support away from us, to dub us conventional chauvinists, fascists, isolationists or just ignorant provincials, and dismiss us.

When we were left to the mercies of the art journals, the professors, and the museum boys, we began immediately to lose influence among the newly budding artists and the young students. The band wagon practitioners, and most artists are unhappily such, left our regionalist banner like rats from a sinking ship and allied themselves with the now dominant internationalisms of the highbrow aesthetes. The fact that these internationalisms were for the most part emanations from cultural events occurring in the bohemias of Paris and thus as local as the forms they deserted never once occurred to any of our band wagon fugitives.

Having long been separated from my teaching contacts, I did not immediately notice the change of student attitude which went with our loss of public attention. But Wood and Curry still maintaining their university positions were much affected and in the course of time under the new indifference, and sometimes actual scorn of the young, began feeling as if their days were over.

It was one of the saddest experiences of my life to watch these two men, so well known and, when compared with most artists, enormously successful, finish their lives in ill health and occasional moods of deep despondency. After the time we came to be publicly associated in the early thirties, we had for all our differences developed a close personal friendship and this loss of self-confidence by my friends was disturbing to me. It was, as a matter of fact, sort of catching and I had more than a few low moments of my own.

Wood and Curry, and particularly Curry, were oversensitive to criticism. They lacked that certain core of inner hardness, so necessary to any kind of public adventure, which throws off the opinions of others when these set up conflicts within the personality. Thus to the profound self-doubts, which all artists of stature experience, was added in these two an unhappy over-susceptibility to the doubts of others. Such a susceptibility in times of despondency or depression is likely to be disastrous. It was most emphatically so for Wood and Curry.

Small men catch the weaknesses of their famous brothers very quickly and in the universities where Wood and Curry taught, there were plenty of these to add their tormenting stings to the mounting uncertainties of my two companions. Oddly enough, although Rita and I tried hard, our friendly encouragements never seemed to equal the discouragements which Wood's and Curry's campus brothers worked up to annoy them. Wood was pestered almost from the beginning of his university career by departmental highbrows who could never understand why an Iowa small towner received world attention while they, with all their obviously superior endowments, received none at all.

By the time we moved over into the forties, both Wood and Curry were in a pretty bad way physically and even psychologically. They had their good moments but these seemed to be rare and shortlived. In the end, what with worry over his weighty debts and his artistic self-doubts, Wood came to the curious idea of changing his identity. Wood was a man of many curious and illusory fancies and when I went to see him in 1942 as he lay dying of a liver cancer in an Iowa hospital, he told me that when he got well he was going to change his name, go where nobody knew him and start all over again with a new style of painting. This was very uncanny because I'm sure he knew quite well he would never come out of that hospital alive. It was as if he wanted to destroy what was in him and become an empty soul before he went out into the emptiness of death. So far as I know Grant had no God to whom he could offer a soul with memories.

John Curry died slowly in 1946 after operations for high blood pressure and a general physical failure had taken his big body to pieces little by little. He made a visit to Martha's Vineyard the Autumn before he died. Sitting before the fire on a cold grey day when a nor'easter was building up seas outside, I tried to bolster his failing spirits.

"John," I ventured, "You must feel pretty good now, after all your struggles, to know that you have come to a permanent place in American art. It's a long way from a Kansas farm to fame like yours."

"I don't know about that," he replied, "maybe I'd have done better to stay on the farm. No one seems interested in my pictures. Nobody thinks I can paint. If I *am* any good, I lived at the wrong time."

This is the way my two famous associates came to their end.

A Note on the Catalogue of Graphics

The works in the catalogue of graphics are listed chronologically, after the works of each artist. When available, each entry contains the following information: catalogue number, title (both a generally accepted and alternate, if applicable), date of composition, medium (primary), dimensions (height by width), edition size, printer, publisher-distributor, locations of impressions, bibliographic references, related works, and supplementary comments. The dates of composition are taken from the prints themselves or from the artists' notes. Therefore, although they are carefully considered, the dates may include inaccuracies. The titles of the works have been taken from the work itself or from the collection that holds the works.

Most of Curry's prints were printed by George Miller. Prints by both artists published and distributed by Associated American Artists were not numbered. Cole numbers, which appear with Curry's lithographs, refer to Sylvan Cole, Jr., *The Lithographs of John Steuart Curry: A Catalogue Raisonné*.

Abbreviations of Collections

AIC – Art Institute of Chicago

Amherst – Amherst College Museum of Art

Bklyn – Brooklyn Museum of Art

BMA – Baltimore Museum of Art

BMAG – Brooks Memorial Art Gallery

Bowdoin – Bowdoin College Museum of Art

BPL – Boston Public Library

CAM – Cincinnati Art Museum

CI – Carnegie Institute, Museum of Art

CMA – Cleveland Museum of Art

Col – Columbus Gallery of Fine Arts, Ohio

Cornell – Cornell University

CRAC – Cedar Rapids Art Center

Dart – Dartmouth College

Dav – Davenport, Iowa, Art Gallery

DIA – Detroit Institute of Arts

DMAC – Des Moines Art Center

Elv – Elevhjem Museum of Art, University of Wisconsin–Madison

FAMSF – Fine Arts Museum of San Francisco

Flint – Flint Institute of Arts

Fogg – Fogg Art Museum, Harvard University

FWMA – Fort Worth Museum of Art

HMA – High Museum of Art

IMA – Indianapolis Museum of Art

Kal – Kalamazoo Art Center

LC – Library of Congress

MFAB – Museum of Fine Arts, Boston

Minn – University of Minnesota

MMA – Metropolitan Museum of Art, New York

MOMA – Museum of Modern Art, New York

N–A – Nelson Gallery–Atkins Museum, Kansas City

NBMA – New Britain Museum of Art

NCFA – National Collection of Fine Arts

NYPL – New York Public Library

Oberlin – Oberlin College Museum of Art

Okl – University of Oklahoma, Norman

PMA – Philadelphia Museum of Art

Princeton – Princeton Museum of Art

RM – Ringling Museum

SFMA – San Francisco Museum of Art

SL – St. Louis Art Museum

Smith – Smith College Museum of Art

SU – Syracuse University

Swarthmore – Swarthmore College

UI – University of Illinois, Krannert Art Museum

UM – University of Michigan

UN – University of Nebraska

UNC – University of North Carolina

WAM – Wichita Art Museum

Wichita – Wichita State University, Edwin A. Ulrich Museum of Art

WM – Whitney Museum of American Art, New York

Yale – Yale University Museum of Art

Bibliography

Primary Sources: The largest collection of letters, photographs, and other documents pertaining to Curry and Wood is in the Archives of American Art, Washington, D.C.

General Sources: Books

Agee, William C. *The 1930's: Painting and Sculpture in America*. New York: Whitney Museum of American Art, 1968.

Baigell, Matthew. *The American Scene: American Painting of the 1930's*. New York: Praeger Publishers, 1974.

———. *Thomas Hart Benton*. New York: Abrams, 1974.

Baur, John I. H. *Revolution and Tradition in Modern American Art*. Cambridge, Mass.: 1951.

Baur, John I. H., ed. *New Art in America*. Greenwich, Conn.: New York Graphic Society, 1951.

Benton, Thomas Hart. *An Artist in America*. Columbia: University of Missouri Press, 1968.

Billington, Ray Allen, ed. *Frontier and Section: Selected Essays of Frederick Jackson Turner*. Englewood Cliffs, N.J.: Prentice-Hall, 1961.

Boswell, Peyton, Jr. *Modern American Painting*. New York: Dodd, Mead, 1939.

Bowen, Howard. *Iowa Income: 1909–1934*. Iowa City: 1935.

Cahill, Holger. *New Horizons in American Art*. New York: Museum of Modern Art, 1936.

———. *American Art Today*. New York: National Art Society, 1939.

Cahill, Holger, and Alfred H. Barr Jr., eds. *Art in America*. New York: Museum of Modern Art, 1934.

Cheney, Martha Chander. *Modern Art in America*. New York: McGraw-Hill, 1939.

Coben, Stanley, and Lorman Ratner, eds. *The Development of an American Culture*. Englewood Cliffs, N.J.: Prentice-Hall, 1970.

Crane, Aimee. *Portrait of America*. New York: The Hyperion Press, 1945.

Craven, Thomas. *Men of Art*. New York: Simon and Schuster, 1934.

Duffus, R. L. *The American Renaissance*. New York: Alfred A. Knopf, 1928.

Ekrich, Arthur A., Jr. *Ideologies and Utopias: The Impact of the New Deal on American Thought*. Chicago: Quadrangle Books, 1969.

Frank, Waldo. *The Rediscovery of America*. New York: Charles Scribner's Sons, 1920.

Goodrich, Lloyd, and John I. H. Baur. *American Art of Our Century*. New York: Praeger Publishers, 1961.

Hagen, Oskar. *The Birth of the American Tradition in Art*. New York: 1940.

Handlin, Oscar. *Truth in History*. Cambridge, Mass.: Belknap Press of Harvard University Press, 1965.

Heller, Nancy, and Julia Williams. *The Regionalists*. New York: Watson-Guptill, 1976.

Hofstadter, Richard. *The Age of Reform: From Bryan to F.D.R.* New York: Alfred A. Knopf, 1955.

———. *Anti-Intellectualism in American Life*. New York: Random House, 1963.

Homer, William Innes. *Robert Henri and His Circle*. Ithaca, N.Y.: Cornell University Press, 1965.

Jensen, Merrill, ed. *Regionalism in America*. Madison: University of Wisconsin Press, 1951.

Jewell, Edward Alden. *Americans*. New York: Alfred A. Knopf, 1930.

———. *Have We an American Art?* New York: Longmans, Green, 1939.

Karanikas, Alexander. *Tillers of a Myth: Southern Agrarians as Social and Literary Critics*. Madison: University of Wisconsin Press, 1966.

Kirschner, Don S. *City and Country: Rural Responses to Urbanization in the Twenties*. Westport, Conn.: 1970.

Leuchtenburg, William E. *Franklin D. Roosevelt and the New Deal*. New York: Harper and Row, 1963.

McKinzie, Richard D. *The New Deal for Artists*. Princeton, N.J.: Princeton University Press, 1973.

McShine, Kynaston, et al. *The Natural Paradise: Painting in America, 1800–1950*. New York: Museum of Modern Art, 1976.

Marx, Leo. *The Machine in the Garden: Technology and the Pastoral Ideal in America*. Oxford: Oxford University Press, 1964.

Nash, Roderick. *Wilderness and the American Mind*. New Haven, Conn.: 1967.

Neuhaus, Eugen. *The History and Ideals of American Art*. Palo Alto, Calif.: Stanford University Press, 1931.

O'Connor, Francis V. *Federal Art Patronage, 1933 to 1945*. Exhibition Catalogue, University of Maryland, College Park, 1966.

———. *Federal Support for the Visual Arts: The New Deal and Now*. Greenwich, Conn.: New York Graphic Society, 1969.

O'Connor, Francis V., ed. *The New Deal Art Projects: An Anthology of Memoirs*. Washington, D.C.: Smithsonian Institution Press, 1972.

O'Doherty, Brian. *American Masters: The Voice and the Myth*. New York: Random House, 1973.

O'Dum, Howard W., and Harry E. Moore. *American Regionalism*. New York: Henry Holt, 1938.

Orton, William Aylott. *American in Search of Culture*. Boston: Little, Brown, 1933.

Overmeyer, Grace. *Government and the Arts*. New York: W. W. Norton and Company, 1939.

Parker, Thomas C. *Frontiers of American Art*. San Francisco: M. H. De Young Memorial Museum, 1939.

Rideout, Walter B. *The Radical Novel in the United States, 1900–1954*. Cambridge, Mass.: Harvard University Press, 1956.

Ringel, Frederick J. *America as Americans See It*. New York: The Literary Guild, 1932.

Rourke, Constance. *The Roots of American Culture*. Edited by Van Wyck Brooks. New York: Harcourt, Brace, 1942.

Saluotos, Theodore, and John D. Hicks. *Agricultural Discontent in the Middle West: 1900–1939*. Madison, Wisconsin: 1951.

Sandler, Irving. *The Triumph of American Painting*. New York: Praeger Publishers, 1970.

Sanford, Charles L. *The Quest for Paradise*. Urbana, Ill.: 1961.

Schlesinger, Arthur M. *New Viewpoints in American History*. New York: Macmillan, 1922.

———. *History of American Life*. New York: Macmillan, 1927–1948.

Shannon, David A. *Twentieth-Century America*. Chicago: 1963.

Smith, Henry Nash. *Virgin Land: The American West as Symbol and*

Myth. New York: Charles Scribner's Sons, 1938.

Stearns, Harold E., ed. *America Now.* New York: Charles Scribner's Sons, 1938.

Susman, Warren, ed. *Culture and Commitment, 1929–1945.* New York: George Braziller, 1973.

Swados, Harvey, ed. *The American Writer and the Great Depression.* Cleveland: Bobbs-Merrill, 1966.

Taine, Hippolyte. *Lectures on Art.* New York: Henry Holt, 1883.

Taylor, Joshua. *America as Art.* Washington, D.C.: Smithsonian Institution Press, 1976.

Watson, Forbes. *American Painting Today.* Washington, D.C.: The American Federation of Art, 1939.

Wecter, Dixon. *The Hero in America.* New York: Charles Scribner's Sons, 1941.

———. *The Age of the Great Depression, 1929–1941.* Chicago: Quadrangle Books, 1971 (first published in 1948).

Wheeler, Monroe. *Painters and Sculptors of Modern America.* New York: Thomas Y. Crowell, 1942.

Wiebe, Robert H. *The Search for Order, 1877–1920.* New York: Hill and Wang, 1967.

Wilmerding, John. *American Art.* New York: Penguin, 1976.

Wilson, Edmund. "The Literary Consequences of the Crash (1932)" in *The Shores of Light.* New York: Farrar, Straus and Young, 1952.

Zevin, B. D., ed. *Nothing to Fear: The Selected Addresses of Franklin Delano Roosevelt, 1932–1945.* Boston: Houghton Mifflin, 1946.

General Sources: Periodicals

"A Portfolio of Posters." *Fortune* 24 (August 1941).

Austin, Mary. "Regionalism in American Fiction." *The English Journal* 21 (January 1932).

Baher, Joseph E. "Regionalism in the Middle West." *The American Review* 4 (March 1935).

Benton, Thomas Hart. "Art and Nationalism." *The Modern Monthly* 8 (May 1934): 232–36.

———. "What's Holding Back American Art?" *Saturday Review of Literature* 34 (15 December 1951): 9–11.

———. "American Regionalism, a Personal History of the Movement." *The University of Kansas City Review* 18 (Autumn 1951).

Botkin, B. A. "Regionalism: Cult or Culture." *The English Journal* 25 (March 1936): 183–84.

Bruce, Edward. "Implications of PWAP." *American Magazine of Art* 27 (March 1934): 113–16.

Craven, Avery. "Frederick Jackson Turner and the Frontier Approach." *The University of Kansas City Review* 18 (Autumn 1951).

Craven, Thomas. "Men in Art: American Style." *The American Mercury* 6 (December 1925): 425–32.

———. "Art and Propaganda." *Scribner's Magazine* 95 (March 1934).

———. "Our Art Becomes American." *Harper's Magazine* 171 (September 1935).

———. "Nationalism in Art." *The Forum* 95 (June 1936).

Davidson, Donald. "Regionalism and Nationalism in American Literature." *The American Review* 5 (April 1935) 48–61.

Dewey, John. "Americanism and Localism." *The Dial* 68 (June 1920).

Janson, H. W. "The International Aspects of Regionalism." *College Art Journal* 2 (May 1943): 110–14.

Jewell, Edward Alden. "Toga Virilis: The Coming of Age of American Art." *Parnassus* 4 (April 1932): 1–3.

———. "Visions That Stir the Mural Pulse." *New York Times* 27 (May 1934).

La Follette, Suzanne. "The Government Recognizes Art." *Scribner's Magazine* 95 (February 1934).

Mangravite, Peippino. "The American Painter and His Environment." *American Magazine of Art* 28 (April 1935).

Mumford, Lewis. "The Theory and Practice of Regionalism." *The Sociological Review* 20 (April 1928).

Suckow, Ruth. "The Folk Idea in American Life." *Scribner's Magazine* 88 (September 1930): 245–55.

Tate, Allen. "Regionalism and Sectionalism." *New Republic* 69 (21 December 1931): 158–60.

"Thomas Hart Benton: An Artist's Selection, 1908–1974." *Nelson Gallery and Atkins Museum Bulletin* 2:2 (1974).

Time (24 December 1934): 24–27.

Warren, Robert Penn. "Some Don'ts for Literary Regionalists." *American Review* 8 (December 1936): 146–50.

John Steuart Curry: Books

Cole, Sylvan, Jr., ed. *The Lithographs of John Steuart Curry: A Catalogue Raisonné.* Introduction by Laurence Schmeckebier. New York: Associated American Artists, 1976.

Madonia, Ann. *Prairie Vision and Circus Wonders: The Complete Lithographic Suite by John Steuart Curry.* Davenport (Iowa) Art Gallery, 1980.

Schmeckebier, Laurence E. *John Steuart Curry's Pageant of America.* New York: American Artists Group, 1943.

John Steuart Curry: Periodicals

Alloway, Lawrence. "The Recovery of Regionalism: John Steuart Curry." *Art in America* (July–August 1976): 70–73.

Benton, Thomas Hart. "Wisconsin Landscape." *Demcourier* (1941): 13–14.

Craven, Thomas. "John Steuart Curry." *Scribner's Magazine* 103 (January 1938).

"Curry Recognized." *Art Digest* 8 (1 September 1934): 7.

Czestochowski, Joseph S. "John Steuart Curry's Lithographs: A Portrait of a Rural America." *American Art Journal* 9:2 (November 1977): 68–82.

"Kansan's Art Sold in East." *Art Digest* 5 (1 August 1931): 6.

Pousette-Dart, Nathaniel. "John Steuart Curry." *Art of Today* 6 (February 1935).

Waller, Bret, et al. "John Steuart Curry." *Kansas Quarterly* 2:4 (Fall 1970).

Wood, Grant. "John Steuart Curry and the Midwest." *Demcourier* 11 (April 1941).

Grant Wood: Books

Batchelder, Ernest A. *Design in Theory and Practice.* New York: 1910.

———. *The Principles of Design.* Chicago: 1904.

Brown, Hazel E. *Grant Wood and Marvin Cone: Artists of an Era.* Ames: Iowa State University Press, 1972.

Dennis, James M. *Grant Wood: A Study in American Art and Culture.* New York: Viking, 1975.

Garwood, Darrell. *Artist in Iowa.* New York: W. W. Norton, 1944.

Liffring-Zug, Joan. *This Is Grant Wood Country.* Davenport (Iowa) Municipal Art Gallery, 1977.

Wood, Grant. *Revolt Against the City.* Iowa City: 1935.

Grant Wood: Periodicals

"*American Gothic*: The Middle West as Depicted by Grant Wood, an American Painter." *London Studio* 4 (July 1932): 34–36.

Batchelder, Ernest A. "How Medieval Craftsmen Created Beauty by Meeting the Constructive Problems of Gothic Architecture." *The Craftsman* 16 (April–September 1909): 44–49.

———. "Carving as an Expression of Individuality: Its Purpose in Architecture." *The Craftsman* 16 (April–September 1909): 60–69.

Boston, Grace. "Stone City Is Ideal for Colony and Art School Planned by Cedar Rapids Artists." *Cedar Rapids Sunday Gazette and Republican* (15 May 1932).

Boswell, Peyton. "Wood, Hard Bitten." *Art Digest* 10 (1 February 1936).

Craven, Thomas. "Grant Wood." *Scribner's Magazine* 101 (June 1937): 21–22.

Cron, Robert. "Iowa Artists Club Forms Art Colony in Deserted Stone City Mansion." *Des Moines Sunday Register* (8 May 1932).

Dennis, James M. "An Essay into Landscapes: The Art of Grant Wood." *Kansas Quarterly* 4:4 (Fall 1972): 12–122.

Doebel, Naomi. "Memorial Window for Island Building Will Be Symbol of Peace and Tribute to Heroic Dead." *Cedar Rapids Gazette* (13 January 1929).

"Fruits of Iowa, Cedar Rapids, The." *American Magazine of Art* 26 (March 1933): 151–52.

"Gertrude Stein Praises Grant Wood." *Montrose (Iowa) Mirror* (17 July 1934).

"Grant Wood Explains Why He Prefers to Remain in Middle West in Talk at Kansas City." *Cedar Rapids Sunday Gazette and Republican* (22 March 1931).

"Grant Wood in the East." *Art Digest* 9 (1 May 1935): 18.

"Iowa Artist Discovers Iowa, An." *Literary Digest* 114 (13 August 1932): 13–14.

"Iowa Cows Give Grant Wood His Best Thoughts." *New York Herald Tribune* (23 January 1936).

"Iowa State University Library Murals." *Fort Dodge (Iowa) Messenger-Chronicle* (17 June 1937).

Jackson, Edna Barnett. "Cedar Rapids' Art Colony, Seed Sown in Turner Alley." *Cedar Rapids Republican* (12 September 1926).

Janson, H. W. "Benton and Wood, Champions of Regionalism." *Magazine of Art* 39 (May 1946).

Kirstein, Lincoln. "An Iowa Memling." *Art Front* 6 (July 1935): 6–8.

Koen, Irma R. "The Art of Grant Wood." *Christian Science Monitor* (26 March 1932).

"Mid-West Is Producing an Indigenous Art." *Art Digest* 7 (1 September 1933): 10.

Pickering, Ruth. "Grant Wood, Painter in Overalls." *North American Review* 240 (September 1935): 271–77.

Rinard, Park. "Grant Wood Restores a Heritage of Charm." *Our Home* 2 (1939): 16–19.

Sayre, Ann H. "Illustrational Work by Grant Wood." *Art News* 34 (25 April 1936): 9.

Sweeney, James Jackson. "Grant Wood." *New Republic* 63 (29 May 1935): 76–77.

Taylor, Adeline. "Easterners Look Wistfully at Midwest as Nation's Art Crown Brought to It: Grant Wood Lionized on New York Visit." *Cedar Rapids Gazette* (12 October 1934).

———. "Cedar Rapids Artist Sponsors Movement for Native Art by Regional Development with Federal Backing." *Cedar Rapids Gazette* (21 October 1934).

Thoma, Margaret. "The Art of Grant Wood." *Demcourier* 12 (May 1942).

Watson, Forbes. "The Phenomenal Professor Wood." *American Magazine of Art* 28 (May 1933).

Whitney, F. A., Jr. "Stone, Steel and Fire: Stone City Comes to Life." *American Magazine of Art* 25 (December 1932): 333–42.

———. "Stone City's Second Season." *American Magazine of Art* 26 (August 1933): 33–39.

"Wood in the Frank Role of Illustrator." *Art Digest* 10 (15 April 1936): 8.

Wood, Grant. "No Trespassing." *The New Country Life* 31 (April 1917): 118.

Index of Illustrations

*Numbers in parentheses indicate location in catalogue raisonné.